ARTISTICALLY AND MUSICALLY TALENTED STUDENTS

Essential Readings in Gifted Education

Series Editor
Sally M. Reis

Enid Zimmerman

EDITOR

ARTISTICALLY AND MUSICALLY TALENTED STUDENTS

A Joint Publication of Corwin Press and the National Association for Gifted Children

ESSENTIAL READINGS IN GIFTED EDUCATION
Sally M. Reis, SERIES EDITOR

CORWIN PRESS
A Sage Publications Company
Thousand Oaks, California

For information:

Corwin Press
A Sage Publications Company
2455 Teller Road
Thousand Oaks, California 91320
www.corwinpress.com

Sage Publications Ltd
1 Oliver's Yard
55 City Road
London EC1Y 1SP
United Kingdom

Sage Publications India Pvt. Ltd.
B-42, Panchsheel Enclave
Post Box 4109
New Delhi 110 017 India

Printed in the United States of America

Library of Congress Cataloging-in-Publication Data

Artistically and musically talented students / Enid Zimmerman, editor.
    p. cm. — (Essential readings in gifted education ; 9)
"A Joint publication of Corwin Press and the National Association for Gifted Children."
Includes bibliographical references and index.
ISBN 978-1-4129-0434-6 (pbk.)
    1. Gifted children—Education—United States. 2. Arts—Study and teaching—United States.
I. Zimmerman, Enid. II. National Association for Gifted Children (U.S.) III. Series.
LC3993.265.A78 2004
371.95'35—dc22

                                        2004001208

This book is printed on acid-free paper.

07   08   10   9   8   7   6   5   4   3   2

Acquisitions Editor:	Kylee Liegl
Editorial Assistant:	Jaime Cuvier
Production Editor:	Sanford Robinson
Typesetter:	C&M Digitals (P) Ltd.
Cover Designer:	Tracy E. Miller
NAGC Publications Coordinator:	Jane Clarenbach

Contents

About the Editors

Sally M. Reis is a professor and the department head of the Educational Psychology Department at the University of Connecticut where she also serves as principal investigator of the National Research Center on the Gifted and Talented. She was a teacher for 15 years, 11 of which were spent working with gifted students on the elementary, junior high, and high school levels. She has authored more than 130 articles, 9 books, 40 book chapters, and numerous monographs and technical reports.

Her research interests are related to special populations of gifted and talented students, including: students with learning disabilities, gifted females and diverse groups of talented students. She is also interested in extensions of the Schoolwide Enrichment Model for both gifted and talented students and as a way to expand offerings and provide general enrichment to identify talents and potentials in students who have not been previously identified as gifted.

She has traveled extensively conducting workshops and providing professional development for school districts on gifted education, enrichment programs, and talent development programs. She is co-author of *The Schoolwide Enrichment Model*, *The Secondary Triad Model*, *Dilemmas in Talent Development in the Middle Years*, and a book published in 1998 about women's talent development titled *Work Left Undone: Choices and Compromises of Talented Females*. Sally serves on several editorial boards, including the *Gifted Child Quarterly*, and is a past president of the National Association for Gifted Children.

Enid Zimmerman has published over 90 articles, 15 book chapters, and co-authored 22 books and monographs including *Art/Design: Communicating Visually*; *Artstrands: A Program for Individualized Art Instruction*; *Women Art Educators I, II, III, IV, V*; *Educating Artistically Talented Students*: *Resources for Educating Artistically Talented Students*: *Understanding Art Testing*; *Issues and Practices Related to Identification of Gifted and Talented Students in the Visual Arts*;

Programming Opportunities for Students Talented in the Visual Arts; and *Research Methods and Methodologies for Art Education.*

Zimmerman was a committee member of the National Art Teacher Exam and consultant to the National Board of Professional Teaching Standards. She was Chair of the National Art Education Association (NAEA) Commission on Research and an International Society for Art Education World Councilor. She received the NAEA Barkan Research Award, the NAEA Women's Caucus Rouse and McFee Awards, and the National Association for Gifted Children's Paper of the Year Award. She was named Indiana Art Educator, NAEA Western Region and Higher Education Division Art Educator, NAEA Distinguished Fellow, NAEA National Art Educator, and the United States Society for Education through Arts Ziegfeld Award. Along with Gilbert Clark, she was recipient of a Javits Gifted and Talented Children's Grant (Project ARTS) from 1994-1997.

Her most recent research projects involve editing a section of the *Handbook of Research and Policy in the Field of Art Education* on teacher education, co-authoring a chapter about artistically talented students, and working with the Hong Kong Department of Education to develop a program for teaching talented art students.

Series Introduction

Sally M. Reis

The accomplishments of the last 50 years in the education of gifted students should not be underestimated: the field of education of the gifted and talented has emerged as strong and visible. In many states, a policy or position statement from the state board of education supports the education of the gifted and talented, and specific legislation generally recognizes the special needs of this group. Growth in our field has not been constant, however, and researchers and scholars have discussed the various high and low points of national interest and commitment to educating the gifted and talented (Gallagher, 1979; Renzulli, 1980; Tannenbaum, 1983). Gallagher described the struggle between support and apathy for special programs for gifted and talented students as having roots in historical tradition—the battle between an aristocratic elite and our concomitant belief in egalitarianism. Tannenbaum suggested the existence of two peak periods of interest in the gifted as the five years following *Sputnik* in 1957 and the last half of the decade of the 1970s, describing a valley of neglect between the peaks in which the public focused its attention on the disadvantaged and the handicapped. "The cyclical nature of interest in the gifted is probably unique in American education. No other special group of children has been alternately embraced and repelled with so much vigor by educators and laypersons alike" (Tannenbaum, 1983, p. 16). Many wonder if the cyclical nature to which Tannenbaum referred is not somewhat prophetic, as it appears that our field may be experiencing another downward spiral in interest as a result of current governmental initiatives and an increasing emphasis on testing and standardization of curriculum. Tannenbaum's description of a valley of neglect may describe current conditions. During the late 1980s, programming flourished during a peak of interest and a textbook on systems and models for gifted programs included 15 models for elementary and secondary programs (Renzulli, 1986). The Jacob Javits Gifted and Talented Students Education Act passed by Congress in 1988 resulted in the creation of the National Research Center on the Gifted and Talented, and dozens of model programs were added to the collective knowledge in the field in areas related to underrepresented populations and successful practices. In the 1990s, reduction or elimination of gifted programs occurred, as budget pressures exacerbated by the lingering recession in the late 1990s resulted in the reduction of services mandated by fewer than half of the states in our country.

Even during times in which more activity focused on the needs of gifted and talented students, concerns were still raised about the limited services provided to these students. In the second federal report on the status of education for our nation's most talented students entitled *National Excellence: A Case for Developing America's Talent* (Ross, 1993), "a quiet crisis" was described in the absence of attention paid to this population: "Despite sporadic attention over the years to the needs of bright students, most of them continue to spend time in school working well below their capabilities. The belief espoused in school reform that children from all economic and cultural backgrounds must reach their full potential has not been extended to America's most talented students. They are under-challenged and therefore underachieve" (p. 5). The report further indicates that our nation's gifted and talented students have a less rigorous curriculum, read fewer demanding books, and are less prepared for work or postsecondary education than the most talented students in many other industrialized countries. Talented children who come from economically disadvantaged homes or are members of minority groups are especially neglected, the report also indicates, and many of them will not realize their potential without some type of intervention.

In this anniversary series of volumes celebrating the evolution of our field, noted scholars introduce a collection of the most frequently cited articles from the premiere journal in our field, *Gifted Child Quarterly*. Each volume includes a collection of thoughtful, and in some cases, provocative articles that honor our past, acknowledge the challenges we face in the present, and provide hopeful guidance for the future as we seek the optimal educational experiences for all talented students. These influential articles, published after a rigorous peer review, were selected because they are frequently cited and considered seminal in our field. Considered in their entirety, the articles show that we have learned a great deal from the volume of work represented by this series. Our knowledge has expanded over several decades of work, and progress has been made toward reaching consensus about what is known. As several of the noted scholars who introduce separate areas explain in their introductions, this series helps us to understand that some questions have been answered, while others remain. While we still search for these answers, we are now better prepared to ask questions that continue and evolve. The seminal articles in this series help us to resolve some issues, while they highlight other questions that simply refuse to go away. Finally, the articles help us to identify new challenges that continue to emerge in our field. Carol Tomlinson suggests, for example, that the area of curriculum differentiation in the field of gifted education is, in her words, an issue born in the field of gifted education, and one that continues to experience rebirth.

Some of the earliest questions in our field have been answered and time has enabled those answers to be considered part of our common core of knowledge. For example, it is widely acknowledged that both school and home experiences can help to develop giftedness in persons with high potential and that a continuum of services in and out of school can provide the greatest likelihood that this development will occur. Debates over other "hot" issues such as grouping and acceleration that took place in the gifted education community 30 years ago are now largely unnecessary, as Linda Brody points out in her introduction to a series of articles in this area. General agreement seems to have been reached, for example, that grouping, enrichment and acceleration are all necessary to provide appropriate educational opportunities for gifted and talented learners. These healthy debates of the past helped to strengthen our field but visionary and reflective work remains to be done. In this series, section editors summarize what has been learned and raise provocative questions about the future. The questions alone are some of the most thoughtful in our field, providing enough research opportunities for scholars for the next decade. The brief introductions below provide some highlights about the series.

DEFINITIONS OF GIFTEDNESS (VOLUME 1)

In Volume 1, Robert Sternberg introduces us to seminal articles about definitions of giftedness and the types of talents and gifts exhibited by children and youth. The most widely used definitions of gifts and talents utilized by educators generally follow those proposed in federal reports. For example, the Marland Report (Marland, 1972) commissioned by the Congress included the first federal definition of giftedness, which was widely adopted or adapted by the states.

The selection of a definition of giftedness has been and continues to be the major policy decision made at state and local levels. It is interesting to note that policy decisions are often either unrelated or marginally related to actual procedures or to research findings about a definition of giftedness or identification of the gifted, a fact well documented by the many ineffective, incorrect, and downright ridiculous methods of identification used to find students who meet the criteria in the federal definition. This gap between policy and practice may be caused by many variables. Unfortunately, although the federal definition was written to be inclusive, it is, instead, rather vague, and problems caused by this definition have been recognized by experts in the field (Renzulli, 1978). In the most recent federal report on the status of gifted and talented programs entitled *National Excellence* (Ross, 1993), a newer federal definition is proposed based on new insights provided by neuroscience and cognitive psychology. Arguing that the term *gifted* connotes a mature power rather than a developing ability and, therefore, is antithetic to recent research findings about children, the new definition "reflects today's knowledge and thinking" (p. 26) by emphasizing talent development, stating that gifted and talented children are children and youth with outstanding talent performance or show the potential for performing at remarkably high levels of accomplishment when compared with others of their age, experience, or environment. These children and youth exhibit high performance capability in intellectual, creative, and/or artistic areas, possess an unusual leadership capacity, or excel in specific academic fields. They require services or activities not ordinarily provided by the schools. Outstanding talents are present in children and youth from all cultural groups, across all economic strata, and in all areas of human endeavor. (p. 26)

Fair identification systems use a variety of multiple assessment measures that respect diversity, accommodate students who develop at different rates, and identify potential as well as demonstrated talent. In the introduction to the volume, Sternberg admits, that just as people have bad habits, so do academic fields, explaining, "a bad habit of much of the gifted field is to do research on giftedness, or worse, identify children as gifted or not gifted, without having a clear conception of what it means to be gifted." Sternberg summarizes major themes from the seminal articles about definitions by asking key questions about the nature of giftedness and talent, the ways in which we should study giftedness, whether we should expand conventional notions of giftedness, and if so, how that can be accomplished; whether differences exist between giftedness and talent; the validity of available assessments; and perhaps most importantly, how do we and can we develop giftedness and talent. Sternberg succinctly summarizes points of broad agreement from the many scholars who have contributed to this section, concluding that giftedness involves more than just high IQ, that it has noncognitive and cognitive components, that the environment is crucial in terms of whether potentials for gifted performance will be realized, and that giftedness is not a single thing. He further cautions that the ways we conceptualize giftedness greatly influences who will have opportunities to develop their gifts and reminds readers of our responsibilities as educators. He also asks one of the most critical questions in our field: whether gifted and talented individuals will use their knowledge to benefit or harm our world.

IDENTIFICATION OF HIGH-ABILITY STUDENTS (VOLUME 2)

In Volume 2, Joseph Renzulli introduces what is perhaps the most critical question still facing practitioners and researchers in our field, that is how, when, and why should we identify gifted and talented students. Renzulli believes that conceptions of giftedness exist along a continuum ranging from a very conservative or restricted view of giftedness to a more flexible or multidimensional approach. What many seem not to understand is that the first step in identification should always be to ask: identification for what? For what type of program or experience is the youngster being identified? If, for example, an arts program is being developed for talented artists, the resulting identification system must be structured to identify youngsters with either demonstrated or potential talent in art.

Renzulli's introductory chapter summarizes seminal articles about identification, and summarizes emerging consensus. For example, most suggest, that while intelligence tests and other cognitive ability tests provide one very important form of information about one dimension of a young person's potential, mainly in the areas of verbal and analytic skills, they do not tell us all that we need to know about who should be identified. These authors do not argue that cognitive ability tests should be dropped from the identification process. Rather, most believe that (a) other indicators of potential should be used for identification, (b) these indicators should be given equal consideration when it comes to making final decisions about which students will be candidates for special services, and (c) in the final analysis, it is the thoughtful judgment of knowledgeable professionals rather than instruments and cutoff scores that should guide selection decisions.

Another issue addressed by the authors of the seminal articles about identification is what has been referred to as the distinction between (a) convergent and divergent thinking (Guilford, 1967; Torrance, 1984), (b) entrenchment and non-entrenchment (Sternberg, 1982), and (c) schoolhouse giftedness versus creative/productive giftedness (Renzulli, 1982; Renzulli & Delcourt, 1986). It is easier to identify schoolhouse giftedness than it is to identify students with the potential for creative productive giftedness. Renzulli believes that progress has been made in the identification of gifted students, especially during the past quarter century, and that new approaches address the equity issue, policies, and practices that respect new theories about human potential and conceptions of giftedness. He also believes, however, that continuous commitment to research-based identification practices is still needed, for "it is important to keep in mind that some of the characteristics that have led to the recognition of history's most gifted contributors are not always as measurable as others. We need to continue our search for those elusive things that are left over after everything explainable has been explained, to realize that giftedness is culturally and contextually imbedded in all human activity, and most of all, to value the value of even those things that we cannot yet explain."

ACCELERATION AND GROUPING, CURRICULUM, AND CURRICULUM DIFFERENTIATION (VOLUMES 3, 4, 5)

Three volumes in this series address curricular and grouping issues in gifted programs, and it is in this area, perhaps, that some of the most promising practices have been implemented for gifted and talented students. Grouping and curriculum interact with each other, as various forms of grouping patterns have enabled students to work on advanced curricular opportunities with other talented students. And, as is commonly known now about instructional and ability grouping, it is not the way students are grouped that matters most, but rather, it is what happens within the groups that makes the most difference.

In too many school settings, little differentiation of curriculum and instruction for gifted students is provided during the school day, and minimal opportunities are offered. Occasionally, after-school enrichment programs or Saturday programs offered by museums, science centers, or local universities take the place of comprehensive school programs, and too many academically talented students attend school in classrooms across the country in which they are bored, unmotivated, and unchallenged. Acceleration, once a frequently used educational practice in our country, is often dismissed by teachers and administrators as an inappropriate practice for a variety of reasons, including scheduling problems, concerns about the social effects of grade skipping, and others. Various forms of acceleration, including enabling precocious students to enter kindergarten or first grade early, grade skipping, and early entrance to college are not commonly used by most school districts.

Unfortunately, major alternative grouping strategies involve the reorganization of school structures, and these have been too slow in coming, perhaps due to the difficulty of making major educational changes, because of scheduling, finances, and other issues that have caused schools to substantially delay major change patterns. Because of this delay, gifted students too often fail to receive classroom instruction based on their unique needs that place them far ahead of their chronological peers in basic skills and verbal abilities and enable them to learn much more rapidly and tackle much more complex materials than their peers. Our most able students need appropriately paced, rich and challenging instruction, and curriculum that varies significantly from what is being taught in regular classrooms across America. Too often, academically talented students are "left behind" in school.

Linda Brody introduces the question of how to group students optimally for instructional purposes and pays particular concern to the degree to which the typical age-in-grade instructional program can meet the needs of gifted students—those students with advanced cognitive abilities and achievement that may already have mastered the curriculum designed for their age peers. The articles about grouping emphasize the importance of responding to the learning needs of individual students with curricular flexibility, the need for educators to be flexible when assigning students to instructional groups, and the need to modify those groups when necessary. Brody's introduction points out that the debate about grouping gifted and talented learners together was one area that brought the field together, as every researcher in the field supports some type of grouping option, and few would disagree with the need to use grouping and accelerated learning as tools that allow us to differentiate content for students with different learning needs. When utilized as a way to offer a more advanced educational program to students with advanced cognitive abilities and achievement levels, these practices can help achieve the goal of an appropriate education for all students.

Joyce VanTassel-Baska introduces the seminal articles in curriculum, by explaining that they represent several big ideas that emphasize the values and relevant factors of a curriculum for the gifted, the technology of curriculum development, aspects of differentiation of a curriculum for the gifted within core subject areas and without, and the research-based efficacy of such curriculum and related instructional pedagogy in use. She also reminds readers of Harry Passow's concerns about curriculum balance, suggesting that an imbalance exists, as little evidence suggests that the affective development of gifted students is occurring through special curricula for the gifted. Moreover, interdisciplinary efforts at curriculum frequently exclude the arts and foreign language. Only through acknowledging and applying curriculum balance in these areas are we likely to be producing the type of humane individual Passow envisioned. To achieve balance, VanTassel-Baska recommends a full set of curriculum options across domains, as well as the need to nurture the social-emotional needs of diverse gifted and talented learners.

Carol Tomlinson introduces the critical area of differentiation in the field of gifted education that has only emerged in the last 13 years. She believes the diverse nature of the articles and their relatively recent publication suggests that this area is indeed, in her words, "an issue born in the field of gifted education, and one that continues to experience rebirth." She suggests that one helpful way of thinking about the articles in this volume is that their approach varies, as some approach the topic of differentiation of curriculum with a greater emphasis on the distinctive mission of gifted education. Others look at differentiation with a greater emphasis on the goals, issues, and missions shared between general education and gifted education. Drawing from an analogy with anthropology, Tomlinson suggests that "splitters" in that field focus on differences among cultures while "lumpers" have a greater interest in what cultures share in common. Splitters ask the question of what happens for high-ability students in mixed-ability settings, while lumpers question what common issues and solutions exist for multiple populations in mixed-ability settings.

Tomlinson suggests that the most compelling feature of the collection of articles in this section—and certainly its key unifying feature—is the linkage between the two areas of educational practice in attempting to address an issue likely to be seminal to the success of both over the coming quarter century and beyond, and this collection may serve as a catalyst for next steps in those directions for the field of gifted education as it continues collaboration with general education and other educational specialties while simultaneously addressing those missions uniquely its own.

UNDERREPRESENTED AND TWICE-EXCEPTIONAL POPULATIONS AND SOCIAL AND EMOTIONAL ISSUES (VOLUMES 6, 7, 8)

The majority of young people participating in gifted and talented programs across the country continue to represent the majority culture in our society. Few doubts exist regarding the reasons that economically disadvantaged, twice-exceptional, and culturally diverse students are underrepresented in gifted programs. One reason may be the ineffective and inappropriate identification and selection procedures used for the identification of these young people that limits referrals and nominations and eventual placement. Research summarized in this series indicates that groups that have been traditionally underrepresented in gifted programs could be better served if some of the following elements are considered: new constructs of giftedness, attention to cultural and contextual variability, the use of more varied and authentic assessments, performance-based identification, and identification opportunities through rich and varied learning opportunities.

Alexinia Baldwin discusses the lower participation of culturally diverse and underserved populations in programs for the gifted as a major concern that has forged dialogues and discussion in *Gifted Child Quarterly* over the past five decades. She classifies these concerns in three major themes: *identification/selection, programming,* and *staff assignment and development.* Calling the first theme **Identification/Selection**, she indicates that it has always been the Achilles' heel of educators' efforts to ensure that giftedness can be expressed in many ways through broad identification techniques. Citing favorable early work by Renzulli and Hartman (1971) and Baldwin (1977) that expanded options for identification, Baldwin cautions that much remains to be done. The second theme, **Programming**, recognizes the abilities of students who are culturally diverse but often forces them to exist in programs designed "for one size fits all." Her third theme relates to **Staffing and Research,** as she voices concerns about the diversity of teachers in these programs as well as the attitudes or mindsets of researchers who develop theories and conduct the research that addresses these concerns.

Susan Baum traces the historical roots of gifted and talented individuals with special needs, summarizing Terman's early work that suggested the gifted were healthier, more popular, and better adjusted than their less able peers. More importantly, gifted individuals were regarded as those who could perform at high levels in all areas with little or no support. Baum suggests that acceptance of these stereotypical characteristics diminished the possibility that there could be special populations of gifted students with special needs. Baum believes that the seminal articles in this collection address one or more of the critical issues that face gifted students at risk and suggest strategies for overcoming the barriers that prevent them from realizing their promise. The articles focus on three populations of students: twice-exceptional students—gifted students who are at risk for poor development due to difficulties in learning and attention;

gifted students who face gender issues that inhibit their ability to achieve or develop socially and emotionally, and students who are economically disadvantaged and at risk for dropping out of school. Baum summarizes research indicating that each of these groups of youngsters is affected by one or more barriers to development, and the most poignant of these barriers are identification strategies, lack of awareness of consequences of co-morbidity, deficit thinking in program design, and lack of appropriate social and emotional support. She ends her introduction with a series of thoughtful questions focusing on future directions in this critical area.

Sidney Moon introduces the seminal articles on the social and emotional development of and counseling for gifted children by acknowledging the contributions of the National Association for Gifted Children's task forces that have examined social/emotional issues. The first task force, formed in 2000 and called the Social and Emotional Issues Task Force, completed its work in 2002 by publishing an edited book, *The Social and Emotional Development of Gifted Children: What Do We Know?* This volume provides an extensive review of the literature on the social and emotional development of gifted children (Neihart, Reis, Robinson, & Moon, 2002). Moon believes that the seminal studies in the area of the social and emotional development and counseling illustrate both the strengths and the weaknesses of the current literature on social and emotional issues in the field of gifted education. These articles bring increased attention to the affective needs of special populations of gifted students, such as underachievers, who are at risk for failure to achieve their potential, but also point to the need for more empirical studies on "what works" with these students, both in terms of preventative strategies and more intensive interventions. She acknowledges that although good counseling models have been developed, they need to be rigorously evaluated to determine their effectiveness under disparate conditions, and calls for additional research on the affective and counseling interventions with specific subtypes of gifted students such as Asian Americans, African Americans, and twice-exceptional students. Moon also strongly encourages researchers in the field of gifted education to collaborate with researchers from affective fields such as personal and social psychology, counseling psychology, family therapy, and psychiatry to learn to intervene most effectively with gifted individuals with problems and to learn better how to help all gifted persons achieve optimal social, emotional, and personal development.

ARTISTICALLY AND CREATIVELY TALENTED STUDENTS (VOLUMES 9, 10)

Enid Zimmerman introduces the volume on talent development in the visual and performing arts with a summary of articles about students who are talented in music, dance, visual arts, and spatial, kinesthetic, and expressive areas. Major themes that appear in the articles include perceptions by parents, students, and teachers that often focus on concerns related to nature versus nurture in arts talent development; research about the crystallizing experiences of artistically talented students; collaboration between school and community members about identification of talented art students from diverse backgrounds; and leadership issues related to empowering teachers of talented arts students. They all are concerned to some extent with teacher, parent, and student views about educating artistically talented students. Included also are discussions about identification of talented students from urban, suburban, and rural environments. Zimmerman believes that in this particular area, a critical need exists for research about the impact of educational opportunities, educational settings, and the role of art teachers on the development of artistically talented students. The impact of the standards and testing movement and its relationship to the education of talented students in the visual and performing arts is an area greatly in need of investigation. Research also is needed about students' backgrounds, personalities, gender orientations, skill development, and cognitive and affective abilities as well as cross-cultural contexts and the impact of global and popular culture on the education of artistically talented students. The compelling case study with which she introduces this volume sets the stage for the need for this research.

Donald Treffinger introduces reflections on articles about creativity by discussing the following five core themes that express the collective efforts of researchers to grasp common conceptual and theoretical challenges associated with creativity. The themes include **Definitions** (how we define giftedness, talent, or creativity), **Characteristics** (the indicators of giftedness and creativity in people), **Justification** (Why is creativity important in education?), **Assessment** of creativity, and the ways we **Nurture** creativity. Treffinger also discusses the expansion of knowledge, the changes that have occurred, the search for answers, and the questions that still remain. In the early years of interest of creativity research, Treffinger believed that considerable discussion existed about whether it was possible to foster creativity through training or instruction. He reports that over the last 50 years, educators have learned that deliberate efforts to nurture creativity are possible (e.g., Torrance, 1987), and further extends this line of inquiry by asking the key question, "What works best, for whom, and under what conditions?" Treffinger summarizes the challenges faced by educators who try to nurture the development of creativity through effective teaching and to ask which experiences will have the greatest impact, as these will help to determine our ongoing lines of research, development, and training initiatives.

EVALUATION AND PUBLIC POLICY (VOLUMES 11, 12)

Carolyn Callahan introduces the seminal articles on evaluation and suggests that this important component neglected by experts in the field of gifted education for at least the last three decades can be a plea for important work by both evaluators and practitioners. She divides the seminal literature on evaluation, and in particular the literature on the evaluation of gifted programs into four categories, those which (a) provide theory and/or practical guidelines, (b) describe or report on specific program evaluations, (c) provide stimuli for the discussion of issues surrounding the evaluation process, and (d) suggest new research on the evaluation process. Callahan concludes with a challenge indicating work to be done and the opportunity for experts to make valuable contributions to increased effectiveness and efficiency of programs for the gifted.

James Gallagher provides a call-to-arms in the seminal articles he introduces on public policy by raising some of the most challenging questions in the field. Gallagher suggests that as a field, we need to come to some consensus about stronger interventions and consider how we react to accusations of elitism. He believes that our field could be doing a great deal more with additional targeted resources supporting the general education teacher and the development of specialists in gifted education, and summarizes that our failure to fight in the public arena for scarce resources may raise again the question posed two decades ago by Renzulli (1980), looking toward 1990: "Will the gifted child movement be alive and well in 2010?"

CONCLUSION

What can we learn from an examination of our field and the seminal articles that have emerged over the last few decades? First, we must **respect the past** by acknowledging the times in which articles were written and the shoulders of those persons upon whom we stand as we continue to create and develop our field. An old proverb tells us that when we drink from the well, we must remember to acknowledge those who dug the well, and in our field the early articles represent the seeds that grew our field. Next, we must **celebrate the present** and the exciting work and new directions in our field and the knowledge that is now accepted as a common core. Last, we must **embrace the future** by understanding that there is no finished product when it comes to research on gifted and talented children and how we are best able to meet their unique needs. Opportunities abound in the work reported in this series, but many questions remain. A few things seem clear. Action in the future should be based on both qualitative and quantitative research as well as longitudinal studies, and what we have completed only scratches the surface regarding the many variables and issues that still need to be explored. Research is needed that suggests positive changes that will lead to more inclusive programs that recognize the talents and gifts of diverse students in our country. When this occurs, future teachers and researchers in gifted education will find answers that can be embraced by educators, communities, and families, and the needs of all talented and gifted students will be more effectively met in their classrooms by teachers who have been trained to develop their students' gifts and talents.

We also need to consider carefully how we work with the field of education in general. As technology emerges and improves, new opportunities will become available to us. Soon, all students should be able to have their curricular needs preassessed before they begin any new curriculum unit. Soon, the issue of keeping students on grade-level material when they are many grades ahead should disappear as technology enables us to pinpoint students' strengths. Will chronological grades be eliminated? The choices we have when technology enables us to learn better what students already know presents exciting scenarios for the future, and it is imperative that we advocate carefully for multiple opportunities for these students, based on their strengths and interests, as well as a challenging core curriculum. Parents, educators, and professionals who care about these special populations need to become politically active to draw attention to the unique needs of these students, and researchers need to conduct the experimental studies that can prove the efficacy of providing talent development options as well as opportunities for healthy social and emotional growth.

For any field to continue to be vibrant and to grow, new voices must be heard, and new players sought. A great opportunity is available in our field; for as we continue to advocate for gifted and talented students, we can also play important roles in the changing educational reform movement. We can continue to work to achieve more challenging opportunities for all students while we fight to maintain gifted, talented, and enrichment programs. We can continue our advocacy for differentiation through acceleration, individual curriculum opportunities, and a continuum of advanced curriculum and personal support opportunities. The questions answered and those raised in this volume of seminal articles can help us to move forward as a field. We hope those who read the series will join us in this exciting journey.

REFERENCES

Baldwin, A.Y. (1977). Tests do underpredict: A case study. *Phi Delta Kappan, 58,* 620-621.

Gallagher, J. J. (1979). Issues in education for the gifted. In A. H. Passow (Ed.), *The gifted and the talented: Their education and development* (pp. 28-44). Chicago: University of Chicago Press.

Guilford, J. E. (1967). *The nature of human intelligence.* New York: McGraw-Hill.

Marland, S. P., Jr. (1972). *Education of the gifted and talented: Vol. 1. Report to the Congress of the United States by the U.S. Commissioner of Education.* Washington, DC: U.S. Government Printing Office.

Neihart, M., Reis, S., Robinson, N., & Moon, S. M. (Eds.). (2002). *The social and emotional development of gifted children: What do we know?* Waco, TX: Prufrock.

Renzulli, J. S. (1978). What makes giftedness? Reexamining a definition. *Phi Delta Kappan, 60*(5), 180-184.

Renzulli, J. S. (1980). Will the gifted child movement be alive and well in 1990? *Gifted Child Quarterly, 24*(1), 3-9. **[See Vol. 12.]**

Renzulli, J. (1982). Dear Mr. and Mrs. Copernicus: We regret to inform you . . . *Gifted Child Quarterly, 26*(1), 11-14. **[See Vol. 2.]**

Renzulli, J. S. (Ed.). (1986). *Systems and models for developing programs for the gifted and talented.* Mansfield Center, CT: Creative Learning Press.

Renzulli, J. S., & Delcourt, M. A. B. (1986). The legacy and logic of research on the identification of gifted persons. *Gifted Child Quarterly, 30*(1), 20-23. **[See Vol. 2.]**

Renzulli J., & Hartman, R. (1971). Scale for rating behavioral characteristics of superior students. *Exceptional Children, 38,* 243-248.

Ross, P. (1993). *National excellence: A case for developing America's talent.* Washington, DC: U.S. Department of Education, Government Printing Office.

Sternberg, R. J. (1982). Nonentrenchment in the assessment of intellectual giftedness. *Gifted Child Quarterly, 26*(2), 63-67. **[See Vol. 2.]**

Tannenbaum, A. J. (1983). *Gifted children: Psychological and educational perspectives.* New York: Macmillan.

Torrance, E. P. (1984). The role of creativity in identification of the gifted and talented. *Gifted Child Quarterly, 28*(4), 153-156. **[See Vols. 2 and 10.]**

Torrance, E. P. (1987). Recent trends in teaching children and adults to think creatively. In S. G. Isaksen (Ed.), *Frontiers of creativity research: Beyond the basics* (pp. 204-215). Buffalo, NY: Bearly Limited.

Introduction to Artistically and Musically Talented Students

Enid Zimmerman

Indiana University

A recent newspaper article about a college student, Kathleen, who received a Rhodes Scholarship to attend Oxford University to complete a master's degree in biochemistry (Denny, 2003), highlighted some of the choices facing talented students. Her long-term goal was to become a medical doctor and conduct research as well as practice medicine. As a very young child, her math skills were outstanding and at age six she played tunes on a piano without ever having taken lessons. By eighth grade she was doing eleventh-grade mathematics and, at age eleven, she was accepted into the Indiana University (IU) School of music to study with a world-renowned pianist. In high school, she practiced the piano four hours a day, studied French, and took biology courses at IU. Her scores on standardized examinations were in the upper one tenth of one percent. Kathleen will graduate with majors in biology, biochemistry, and music, with a minor in French. A professor at IU introduced her to the world of medical research and one summer she spent nine weeks in New York City studying in the field of molecular pharmacology. When asked about her successes, she attributed her success to many people including her parents who offered her support and encouragement. Her mother made sure lessons and experiences she needed were accessible to her, and her father, a mathematics professor, transported her to different activities. A high school guidance counselor and two IU professors "played significant roles in shaping her life" (Denny, 2003, p. A2). She said, "I felt things deeply, and became upset by human suffering that's occurred throughout history. . . . I expressed my thoughts and feelings in journals, and poems, and I decided that I really wanted to make a difference in this world" (Denny, 2003, p. 7).

This student's story reflected some of the issues raised in the articles published in the series. Her many talents, support from teachers and parents, a burning desire to master several academic and arts areas in school curriculum, and her dedication and desire to make a difference in the world are all indications of her gifts and talents. The eight articles about talent development in the visual and performing arts are both qualitative and quantitative and include three about music, one about dance and music, three about visual art talent, and one about spatial, kinesthetic, expressive, and music talent development. Major themes that appear in the eight articles include perceptions by parents, students, and teachers that often focus on concerns related to nature versus nurture in arts talent development; research about crystallizing experiences experienced by artistically talented students; collaboration between school and community members about identification of talented art students from diverse backgrounds; and leadership issues related to empowering teachers of talented arts students.

A SUMMARY OF THE CONTENT OF THE ARTICLES

In the first article, "Decisions Regarding Music Training: Parental Beliefs and Values," Dai and Schader (2002) discussed beliefs and values that motivated parents to support their children's music education. A questionnaire was used to access parents' expectancy and value beliefs in areas of music, academics, and athletics, and perceptions of their children's abilities and talent, motivation, and effort and the importance of success. Participants were parents of students between the ages of six and eighteen who were attending programs at four prestigious music institutions in large cities across the United States. This was not a typical population, as almost half these parents had played musical instruments, a majority of them were well educated, and many were first-generation Americans from diverse backgrounds.

Results indicated a high correlation between age and years of music lessons; with advancing age and more years of training, parents are more likely to coordinate their aspirations with perceptions of their children's strengths and motivation. Parents believed in the potential of their children in both music and academic areas, but seemed to value music and academic achievement more than athletic achievement. With increasing years of music training, the more parents become single-minded in their achievement aspirations for their children. Parents' perceptions of music success for their children (including ability and motivation) appeared to be crucial for continuing support of their children's music development. Parents sent their children for music training, not for music talent development; however, after some advanced training was completed, parent support for sustained engagement in music training became increasingly important.

Evans, Bickel, and Pendarvis (2000) also focused on perceptions of music talent, and the nature versus nurture controversy that is a salient issue in arts talent development. This study compared students' attributions regarding the source of their music accomplishments with their parents' and teachers' attribution patterns. The study was conducted in a music camp and the vast majority of students were white, from middle and upper middle-class backgrounds, and had well-educated parents. Student, parent, and teacher questionnaires were developed to solicit information about identifying similarities in attribution patterns about the nature versus nurture issue. Findings suggest that students were convinced they had innate music talent and thought their teachers and friends shared this point of view, but some viewed their teachers and friends as discouraging their music talent development. They reported experiencing early exposure and music involvement, worked long and hard on their musical growth, and received in-school encouragement. Some parents believed that hard work might lead to disappointment, frustration and self-defeat. Parents also believed that early exposure and encouragement offered by family and friends, along with students' own disposition to work, accounted for the music development in spite of a lack in innate ability. Teachers attributed music accomplishments to innate talent, interest, exposure, involvement, and hard work but did not include the influence of family and friends. Interestingly, all attributions tended to be self-serving. Parents regarded their own contributions through encouragement and providing opportunities for involvement in music as crucial to their children's music development. Teachers regarded schoolwork and rewards garnered in school as important influences in their students' music talent development. Students regarded their own ability and hard work as sources of success.

Many different opinions exist in the arts talent development literature about precocity and how it is manifested in student development. Freeman (1999) focused on sudden insights that set a person's life on course and dramatically effect that person's view of his or her ability within a given domain. She tried to investigate whether crystallizing experiences were a common occurrence in musically precocious boys and to explore the nature of those experiences. Student interviews, focus groups, and parental discussions were conducted at a choir school for boys in New York City. The majority were White students from upper-middle-class families with strong academic backgrounds and demonstrated talent in voice and instrumental domains. Freeman determined that crystallizing experiences were common phenomena among these musically precocious students. In this study, it appears that parental support and early instruction are more important than innate talent and that talent is necessary but not sufficient for exceptional achievement in music. Others (Haroutounian, 2002) also have found that innate ability, practice, and hard work, along with support and encouragement of parents who themselves have musical backgrounds are important ingredients for art talent to flow. If crystallizing experiences can lead to attaining personal goals, Freeman (1999) poses a critical question about whether such experiences help music talents to be actualized.

Baum, Owen, and Oreck (1996) studied urban students who are economically disadvantaged or do not do well on written tests and are not often identified as having outstanding dance or music talents. The researchers explained that auditions have little predictive validity for students who have little opportunity for, or exposure to formal training in the arts. They attempted to adapt means for reducing cultural and socio-economic biases to identify third-graders from diverse populations in two New York City schools with a substantial percentage of bilingual and special education students. Based on Renzulli's (1977) Three Ring Conception of Giftedness, which includes above-average ability, creativity, and task commitment, the researchers developed an observational model with checklists for screening students with high potential dance and music talents. All students at the two schools were observed and then some students were chosen to participate in a seven-week, multi-session audition class. Some who evidenced high potential were chosen for even more advanced lessons. Student successes in national and international arenas are presented as evidence of the success of the processes and instruments the authors developed to identify students they considered at risk. The authors believe experiences in the arts helped to reverse failure in academic environments.

Kay and Subotnik's (1994) article is linked to the previous article. Gardner's (1983) theory of multiple intelligences (musical, spatial, and kinesthetic) and Renzulli's (1977, 1986) Three Ring Conception were modified to include physical and cognitive skills in music and dance, motivation, and creativity that was defined as individual expression and cooperative problem solving. The authors contended that dance and music instruction need to begin at an early age, yet there are few such programs at the elementary level. Students in this study were from diverse cultural, ethnic, and socioeconomic backgrounds. As in the Baum, Owen, and Oreck study (1996), an extended seven-week audition process was developed to expose all students in grades three and four in two urban schools in New York City to art forms and related skills, from which students could then be identified. After the identification process, the programs offered long-term, in-depth curriculum modification for selected students.

Qualitative data, collected through onsite visits, observations, and interviews, determined that as a result of this project, teachers reported being able to identify a wide range of talent among students and see value in integrating the arts into elementary education curricula. The researchers also found that students with motivation and creativity could be taught the basic skills, but students who came with basic skills had a harder time developing creatively.

Clark and Zimmerman (2001) focused on artistically talented visual arts students in rural schools from economically disadvantaged and/or ethnically diverse backgrounds. Project ARTS was a three-year project, funded by a Javits grant, to identify underserved, high ability, visual and performing students in grade three for implementation and assessment of differentiated visual arts programs appropriate to these same students in the next two years. Two rural schools serving rural culturally diverse students in New Mexico, two in Indiana, and three schools in South Carolina participated in Project ARTS. Locally designed measures in the visual and performing arts were used to identify students with potential talents in the hopes that enriching experiences would to help them develop advanced products. Two standardized instruments, Clark's Drawing Abilities Test (CDAT) and an abbreviated Torrance Tests of Creative Thinking (TTCT) were used and a correlation was found between CDAT and TTCT even though they measure different expectations, executions, product outcomes, completion, and scoring criteria. Students who were higher achieving in other content areas also had higher achievement in the visual arts than those who were lower achieving in other content areas. The locally designed measures were found to be appropriate for identifying artistically talented students in their local schools. A number of different measures was recommended be used for identification that include different several local measures, CDAT, and achievement test scores.

Similar to the Evans, Bickel, and Pendarvis (2000) article, students' perceptions about being artistically talented was the focus of another article co-authored by Clark and Zimmerman (1988) with artistically talented students. Most students were aware of their art talents and had favorable views of themselves as well as gifted students in general. These students reported having "illuminating experiences" that were similar to, but less intense than, those reported by Freeman (1999). Their art-making experiences were stimulated by pleasurable experiences, not emotional crises, and they devoted much time and energy to doing artwork. Family members were viewed as encouraging art talent development even if they did not have art backgrounds or many resources in their homes that encouraged art study. Many of these students also expressed a need for advanced teachers who would challenge them more than they were experiencing in many of their school situations.

One article (Zimmerman, 1997) addressed the topic of professional development for teachers of artistically talented students. Few studies exist about developing leadership and empowerment of students talented in the visual and performing arts. A survey of past participants and a focus group of teachers attending one summer session were conducted. Content analysis of responses to a questionnaire and focus group interview questions resulted in categories that included knowledge of subject matter and pedagogy, self-esteem, collaboration, and empowerment. It appeared knowledge of subject matter content and pedagogy, building self-esteem, and allowing choices lead teachers to take leadership roles and collaborate with others. Eventually they made changes in their private and professional lives in their schools, communities, state organizations, and beyond, and became activists for promoting appropriate education for artistically talented students.

REFLECTIONS ON THEMES IN THE ARTICLES

In considering Kathleen's case presented earlier, it is evident she possessed many qualities normally associated with a student who is gifted and talented in both the areas of music and academics. Her parents are well educated and she displayed high levels of talent at an early age. Her parents were supportive and encouraged her abilities, although neither were musicians. In addition, she participated in extracurricular activities and in special college level programs when she was in high school. Several of her teachers were role models and provided contexts for her illuminating experiences that led to her success and dedication to make a difference in the world. How unique is her case and how does it relate to the articles in this section?

There were many similarities and differences in these articles. Researchers all collected data from special programs designed for artistically talented music and visual arts students. In several studies, parent and community involvement was important to the success of the programs. Similar findings emerged about hard work, parental support, and differentiated curriculum as necessary for developing arts talents. Identification procedures that were developed did not rely solely on standardized test scores and, in a number of studies, local measures were devised that emphasized observation, performance, work samples, and recommendations from a variety of sources.

Common to the articles about music talent development were notions that supported research and assumptions in the work of Bloom, Renzulli, and Gardner. Bloom (1985) and his colleagues examined processes by which individuals reach high levels of accomplishment in their fields by the age of 35 and their findings were referred to in several studies in this section. Several music and dance studies adapted Renzulli's (1977) Three Ring Model of Giftedness. Gardner's (1983) theory of Multiple Intelligences was an important basis for the research in several dance and music articles. Although there were many commonalities found in the articles in this section, there were a variety of differences as well.

The studies in this section represent diverse students, parents, and teachers from suburban, inner city environments; rural contexts; and various socioeconomic groups. Students at both elementary and secondary schools were included in the studies. Several researchers who conducted inquiries in inner-city schools claimed that dance and music success does not correlate with a history of academic success, but at the same time believed that positive experiences in the arts could reverse failure in academic environments. These researchers claimed that identification in their program was based on audition performances, rather than on factors such as classroom behavior, ethnicity, or academic scores and that their procedures were free of cultural and economic bias. On the other hand, other studies took place in rural areas and small cities with diverse populations and produced data that indicated high achievement in the visual arts is most likely to be accomplished by students who are high achieving in other school subjects. These differences in findings bring to light problems that involve using outcomes from one study in a particular context and claiming that they can be generalized to other contexts with vastly different populations of students.

One topic of concern that was not addressed in most of the studies was gender differences in art talent development. In a study I conducted (Zimmerman, 1995) about differences between artistically talented boys and girls, cultural stereotyping was apparent in choices of subject matter and media, awareness of their capabilities in art, and practical planning for future careers as artists. I suggested that counselors, parents, teachers, and community members should be educating artistically talented girls to be independent, have a mission in their lives, develop strong senses of identity and self-esteem, and achieve in contexts free of sexual stereotypes or negative influences.

Diverse research methods were used in articles in this section, including both qualitative and quantitative methodologies for collecting and interpreting data. Use of a variety of methods is important and ensures the quality of inquiry in the field of gifted and talented arts education with a broad base of support in the field of educational research. Without in-depth inquiry, one time, idiosyncratic studies may produce misconceptions that have been widely proliferated and accepted by the public at large. In-depth lines of inquiry do exist in arts education. For example, a theoretical model has been developed about art teacher leadership development and artistically talented students that represents the culmination of a decade of collaboration researching feminism and leadership in art education (Thurber & Zimmerman, 1997, 2002; Zimmerman, in press).

MISCONCEPTIONS AND MISUNDERSTANDINGS ABOUT ARTS TALENT DEVELOPMENT

Many educators assume that composing, playing an instrument, and singing requires natural talent and that innate talent in music and the visual arts is the most important factor needed to be successful in the arts. However, not all students have music talent (Davis, 1994). In fact, Sosniak (1985) and Sloan and Sosniak (1985) reported in Bloom's (1985) classic book about talent development that objective accounts of early music and art talent did not point toward innate giftedness in those areas.

Parents in two studies about music talent viewed potential in their children based not only on natural talent, but also on their children's motivational levels and their own contributions of encouragement and support (Dai & Schader, 2002; Evans, Bickel, & Pendarvis, 2000). Teachers found schoolwork and rewards influential in developing music talent, whereas students attributed their talent and success to hard work (Evans, Bickel, & Pendarvis, 2000). Findings from a study by Guskin, Zimmerman, Okolo, and Peng (1986), conducted with academic and visual arts students, suggested both groups of students wanted gifts and talents to be the result of effort, rather than some immutable difference.

Another widely held misconception is that the development of visual art and performing art talents are similar to each other but are quite different from development in traditionally academic subjects. Haroutounian (2002) believes music talent is different from visual arts talent and that generalized arts rating scales should not be used because they tend to link the arts as one entity. In 1989, Gardner argued that there is not a separate artistic intelligence but rather each intelligence can be "directed toward artistic ends; that is, the symbols may, but need not be marshaled in an artistic fashion" (p. 74). Music educators, including those whose articles are included in this section, have embraced Gardner's concept of musical intelligence as an important theoretical conception. In the visual arts, there is no groundswell of support perhaps because there is no identified visual arts intelligence in Gardner's approach.

Another difference between music talent development and visual arts talent development is the manifestation of extraordinary talent at an early age. Prodigious behavior is evident in music and chess but there have been few prodigies in visual arts. Seashore (1938) and Gordon (1989) confirmed that basic music qualities are displayed at an early age and reliable measurement of music talent can be made by age 9 or 10. Walters and Gardner (1984) claimed musical and mathematical talent would emerge at earlier ages than talent in the visual arts. Others claim students will manifest talent in the arts at different ages or grade levels (Bloom, 1985; Khatena, 1989). Early talent development seems to be more of an established notion in music education and is not as much a fixed concept in visual arts education.

Either tacitly expressed or directly stated, it is a widely held belief by educators and others that students in the arts are not outstanding academically, in fact they have problems in academic subjects. Some research reported in these articles indicates that students who were talented in dance and music were less successful in some academic subjects (Baum, Owen, & Oreck, 1996). Two studies in this section concluded that some artistically talented visual arts students also were accomplished in academic subjects as well (Clark & Zimmerman, 1988, 2001). More research needs to be done in this area.

Scholars have questioned the arbitrary separation of intelligence and arts performance for many years. Gardner (1983) claimed a positive relationship among the arts and intellectual and academic abilities, whereas Sternberg (1985) argued that art abilities are not related to intellectual capabilities. Winner (1996) suggested that artistically talented students have abilities that cannot be measured on a traditional IQ test. Eisner (1994) claimed that affect and cognition are *not* independent processes that can be separated. Cognition is expanded through different kinds of intelligence as people confront and solve problems.

Another common misconception held by many educators is that creativity is a mutually understood term in visual and performing arts talent development. Several of the studies in this section about musical and dance talent development used creativity, derived from Renzulli's (1977) Three Ring Conception, as part of a definition leading to an identification procedure. Several researchers in this section modified Renzulli's definition of creativity so that it could be operationalized in their studies. In the Baum, Owen, and Oreck (1996) study, creativity itself is not defined, but it is operationalized as expressiveness, movement qualities, improvisation in dance and expressiveness composition, and improvisation in music. In the Kay and Subotnik (1994) article, creativity was conceived as individual expression and cooperative problem solving in music and dance using the same categories for creativity as in the Baum, Owen, and Oreck (1996) article. Although Zimmerman and Clark (2001) found a correlation between Clark's Drawing Ability Test and Torrance's Test of Creative Thinking, Torrance (1963) himself reported that creative achievements in writing, science, medicine, and leadership were more easily predicted than creative achievements in music, the visual arts, business, or industry. Haroutounian (2002), in her book about music talent development, advised that music educators not use general creativity tests, aptitude or IQ tests, or academic achievement tests as measures for identifying artistically talented students. They are not suitable for arts identification, she contended, and may exclude potentially talented arts students.

As is evident in educational and psychological literature, there is no agreement among the terms *talent*, *giftedness*, and *creativity* and relationships among these terms. Sternberg and Lubart's (1999) definition of creativity as "the ability to produce work that is both novel . . . and appropriate" (p. 3) is one that has been widely accepted. A number of contemporary psychologists and educators also agree that creativity is a complex process that can be viewed as an interactive system in which relationships among person, process, products, and social and cultural contexts is of paramount importance (Csikszentmihalyi, 1996; Sternberg 1999).

Contexts in which students are judged to be creative can vary from one setting to another. Sternberg (2001) viewed intelligence in a dialectical relationship to creativity, where intelligence is viewed as advancing societal norms and creativity as opposing societal norms and proposing new norms. A person needs intelligence to be creative, therefore, but not all intelligent people are creative. Creativity from this point of view is a characteristic of an individual as he or she reacts with one or more systems within a particular social context.

A number of researchers claim that only adults can be creative. For example, children, according to Csikszentmihalyi (1996), can demonstrate talent in a number of areas, but they cannot be creative because creativity involves changing a domain and the ways of thinking within that domain. Other researchers, however, have supported the position that nearly everyone has some creative ability and their potential should be supported in educational settings (Parkhurst, 1999). From this point of view, creativity would then encompass what is creative for a student in a particular school context, rather than the society in which the student resides.

SOME CONCLUDING THOUGHTS

To enable students such as Kathleen, whose accomplishments were described earlier, to make a difference in this world, research must be conducted that addresses important issues in the fields of visual and performing arts talent development. A research agenda should be developed that can provide important information for improving educational opportunities for talented arts students. These articles represent the work of a number of researchers who are conducting inquiry in the field of developing talent in the areas of music, dance, and the visual arts. More research is needed in drama education as well. In addition, there is a need for research about the impact of educational opportunities, educational settings, and the role of art teachers on the development of artistically talented students. The impact of the standards and testing movement and its relationship to the education of talented students in the visual and performing arts is an area greatly in need of investigation. Research also is needed about male and female students' backgrounds, personalities, skill development, and cognitive and affective abilities as well as cross-cultural contexts and the impact of global and popular culture on the education of artistically talented students.

REFERENCES

Baum, S. M., Owen, S. V., & Oreck, B. A. (1996). Talent beyond words: Identification of potential talent in dance and music in elementary students. *Gifted Child Quarterly, 40*(2), 93-101. **[See Vol. 9, p. 57.]**

Bloom, B. S. (1985). *Developing talent in young people.* New York: Ballantine.

Clark, G., & Zimmerman, E. (1988). Views of self, family background, and school: Interviews with artistically talented students. *Gifted Child Quarterly, 32*(4), 340-346. **[See Vol. 9, p. 103.]**

Clark, G., & Zimmerman, E. (2001). Identifying artistically talented students in four rural communities in the United States. *Gifted Child Quarterly, 45*(2), 104-114. **[See Vol. 9, p. 83.]**

Csikszentmihalyi, M. (1996). *Creativity: Flow and the psychology of discovery and invention.* New York: HarperCollins.

Dai, D. Y., & Schader, R. M. (2002). Decisions regarding music training: Parental beliefs and values. *Gifted Child Quarterly, 46*(2), 135-144. **[See Vol. 9, p. 1.]**

Davis, M. (1994). Folk music psychology. *Psychologist, 7*(12), 537.

Denny, D. (2003, January 20). New challenge awaits top student: Rhodes scholarship. *The Herald Times,* pp. A1, A2, A7.

Eisner, E. W. (1994). *Cognition and curriculum reconsidered.* New York: Teachers College Press.

Evans, R. J., Bickel, R., & Pendarvis, E. D. (2000). Musical talent: Innate or acquired? Perceptions of students, parents, and teachers. *Gifted Child Quarterly, 44*(2), 80-90. **[See Vol. 9, p. 19.]**

Freeman, C. (1999). The crystallizing experience: A study in musical precocity. *Gifted Child Quarterly, 43* (2), 75-85. **[See Vol. 9, p. 39.]**

Gardner, H. (1983). *Frames of mind: The theory of multiple intelligences*. New York: Basic Books.

Gardner, H. (1989). Zero-based arts education: An introduction to ARTS PROPEL. *Studies in Art Education, 30* (2), 71-83.

Gordon, E. (1989). Advanced measures of music audiation. Chicago: GIA.

Guskin, S., Zimmerman, E., Okola, C., & Peng, J. (1986). Being labeled gifted or talented: Meanings and effects perceived by students in special programs. *Gifted Child Quarterly, 30*(2), 61-65.

Haroutounian, J. (2002). *Kindling the spark: Recognizing and developing musical talent*. New York: Oxford University Press.

Kay, S. L., & Subotnik, R. F. (1994). Talent beyond words: Unveiling spatial, expressive, kinesthetic, and musical talent in young children. *Gifted Child Quarterly, 38*(2), 70-74. **[See Vol. 9, p. 73.]**

Khatena, J. (1989). Intelligence and creativity to multitalent. *Journal of Creative Behavior, 23*(2), 93-97.

Lubart, T. L. (1999). Creativity across cultures. In R. Sternberg (Ed.), *Handbook of creativity* (pp. 339-350). Cambridge, UK: Cambridge University Press.

Parkhurst, H. B. (1999). Confusion, lack of consensus, and the definition of creativity as a construct. *Journal of Creative Behavior, 33*(1), 1-21.

Renzulli, J. S. (1977). *The enrichment triad model: A guide for developing defensible programs for the gifted and talented*. Mansfield Center, CT: Creative Learning Press.

Renzulli, J. S. (1986). The three-ring conception of giftedness: A developmental model for creative productivity. In R. J. Sternberg & J. E. Davidson (Eds.), *Conceptions of giftedness* (pp. 53-92). New York: Cambridge University Press.

Seashore, C.E. (1938). *Psychology of music*. New York: McGraw-Hill.

Sloan, K.D., & Sosniak, L.A. (1985). The development of accomplished sculptors. In B. Bloom (Ed.), *Developing talent in young people* (pp. 90-138). New York: Ballantine.

Sosniak, L.A. (1985). Learning to be a concert pianist. In B. Bloom (Ed.), *Developing talent in young people* (pp. 19-67). New York: Ballantine Books.

Sternberg, R. J. (1985). *Beyond IQ: A triarchic theory of human intelligence*. New York: Cambridge University Press.

Sternberg, R. J. (Ed.). (1999). *Handbook of creativity*. Cambridge, UK: Cambridge University Press.

Sternberg, R. J. (2001). What is the common thread of creativity? *American Psychologist, 56* (4), 360-362.

Sternberg, R. J., & Lubart, T. I. (1999). Concept of creativity: Prospects and paradigms. In R. J. Sternberg (Ed.), *Handbook on creativity* (pp. 3-15). New York: Cambridge University Press.

Thurber, F., & Zimmerman, E. (1997). Voice to voice: Developing in-service teachers' personal, collaborative, and public voices. *Educational Horizons, 75*(4), 20-26.

Thurber, F., & Zimmerman, E. (2002). An evolving feminist leadership model for art education. *Studies in Art Education, 44* (1), 5-27.

Torrance, E. P. (1963). *Education and creative potential*. Minneapolis, MN: University of Minnesota Press.

Walters, J., & Gardner, H. (1984, March). *The crystallizing experience: Discovering an intellectual gift*. Technical paper, supported by grants from the Social Science Research Council and the Bernard van Leer Foundation of The Hague.

Winner, E. (1996). *Gifted children: Myths and realities*. New York: Basic Books.

Zimmerman, E. (1995). Factors influencing the art education of artistically talented girls. *The Journal of Secondary Gifted Education, 6*(2), 103-112.

Zimmerman, E. (1997). I don't want to sit in the corner cutting out valentines: Leadership roles for teachers of talented art students. *Gifted Child Quarterly, 41*(1), 37-41. **[See Vol. 9, p. 119.]**

Zimmerman, E. (in press). I don't want to stand out there and let my underwear show: Leadership experiences of seven former women doctoral students. In. K. Grauer, R. Irwin, & E. Zimmerman (Eds.), *Women art educators V: Conversations across time—remembering, revisioning, reconsidering.* Montreal, Canada: Canadian Society for Education through Art.

1

Decisions Regarding Music Training: Parental Beliefs and Values

David Yun Dai

State University of New York at Albany

Robin M. Schader

University of Connecticut

Musical talent development generally involves high levels of parental support over an extended period of time. This study examined parents' expectancy beliefs and values regarding their child's music training, regular academic work, and athletic activities. Parents of 231 students, aged 6–18, who attended programs at four music institutions responded to a questionnaire. The results suggest that parents may initially send their children for music training not for musical talent development per se, but for more general educational value. However, with more training and

Editor's Note: From Dai, D. Y., & Schader, R. M. (2002). Decisions regarding music training: Parental beliefs and values. *Gifted Child Quarterly, 46*(2), 135-144. © 2002 National Association for Gifted Children. Reprinted with permission.

more advanced musical development, parents seem to regulate their beliefs and values across the three domains in the single-minded service of musical talent development.

T he prolonged process of musical talent development is highly demanding in terms of financial resources and time investment. In addition, a supportive home environment is considered essential. Freeman (1976) found that children who were encouraged to try a musical instrument in school often gave it up if their home environment was not sufficiently supportive. In a more recent study, Davidson, Howe, Moore, and Sloboda (1996) conducted interviews with the parents of more than 250 children engaged in instrumental music study and found that parents' interest in music and involvement in their children's music training was associated with whether or not their children would continue music lessons and practice. It seems that parents play a critical role in initiating and sustaining children's music training over a substantial period of time, and their involvement may be essential for musical talent to flourish. In this study, we investigated musical development from the parents' perspective and explored the beliefs and values that motivated parents to support their children's music training.

PARENTS' EXPECTANCY BELIEFS AND ATTRIBUTIONS

Ericsson, Tesch-Romer, and Krampe (1990) suggested that, if parents and their children invest a great deal in an activity, often at the expense of other options and interests, they must be confident that potential for success in the activity is high. One source of such confidence is parents' perceptions of musical ability or talent in their children (Davidson et al., 1996). For this reason, parents' perceptions of their children's musical talent may be an important factor in the decision to continue music training for a substantial period of time. Parents' expectancy beliefs can influence their children's self-perceptions of musical competence, as well as the parents' own levels of involvement and motivation. There is substantial research evidence suggesting that parental beliefs in children's competencies and talents contribute to children's related self-perceptions (Frome & Eccles, 1998; Parsons, Adler, & Kaczala, 1982; Phillips, 1987; see Dix, 1993, for a review). However, Evans, Bickel, and Pendarvis (2000) suggested, based on their study, that parents tend to discount the musical giftedness of their children as a major contributor to their achievement and success in music. Parents of young pianists in Sosniak's (1997) study also did not feel that their eminent pianist children were particularly talented in their early years. Thus, whether parents have different views of the importance of ability as related to success in a specific area needs to be further investigated.

Putting the Research to Use

Contrary to our assumption, most parents do not espouse long-term goals for their children's musical development. It is only when their children have entered high school, moved to more advanced levels of music training, or both that parents seem to face important choices and potential conflicts. Parents' strong beliefs about their children's musical potential and high aspirations for their children's musical achievement may be necessary for sustaining music training at advanced levels. Parents do not seem to differentiate talent and motivation, ability and effort to the extent their children do. A view of musical talent as a dynamic, malleable quality, rather than a static trait, typically enhances motivation, though such a view can also result in conflicting attributions, as parents and their children may interpret success and failure in music training differently.

Beyond ability, development of musical competence requires effort or hard work for a prolonged period of time (Ericsson, Krampe, & Tesch-Romer, 1993; Sloboda, Davidson, Howe, & Moore, 1996; Sosniak, 1997). How do parents perceive the effort demands of musical development and how do they perceive the motivational and personality characteristics of their children that may either facilitate or impede high-level effort? These perceptions may derive from parents' daily observations, but they are also likely to have subjective biases. No matter what foundation, these perceptions can also influence parents' levels of involvement and decisions as to whether music training for their children is a worthwhile investment and will bear fruit in the long run.

What if children have multiple interests and potentialities that compete for limited time and resources? The issue of multipotentialities, or what Gagné (1999) called *polyvalence*, is relevant for most musically inclined children. Not only is good academic performance a prerequisite for conventional pathways to success, but extracurricular activities such as athletics are also seen as highly popular and inviting. Are parents more open to a variety of options when they perceive multiple potentialities in their child? Do parents who perceive music training as demanding in terms of time and effort see a conflict between and among musical, academic, and athletic demands? Kemp (1996) found that musically inclined children tended to be introverted. Based on this finding, one would speculate that these children might be less interested in athletic activities, which often require teamwork and social interaction.

Parents' Value Beliefs

If success in music is likely, but not considered important, investment is pointless. This leads to the value issue, that is, how important is music to parents? The degree of importance in an activity or pursuit is always relative to the importance of other available options and opportunities. How do parents prioritize competing demands and opportunities in their children's lives? Given the fact that effort in conventional academic areas may lead to more lucrative careers than music, do parents try to balance the two areas to keep options open? Do they experience ambivalent feelings toward music training?

Developmental Changes in Parents' Expectancy and Value Beliefs

From a developmental point of view, parent perceptions and value beliefs may depend to a great degree on the child's stage of musical development. Bloom and his colleagues (Bloom, 1985; Sosniak, 1997) identified three phases of talent development in childhood and adolescence. In the first phase, playful interaction with the domain, be it music, athletics, or mathematics, is encouraged. Teachers and parents do not emphasize external criteria for performance or achievement. The second phase includes involvement in a more systematic acquisition of knowledge and skills under the supervision of teachers and parents. More rigorous standards are used to evaluate the progress the child is making. With heightened expectations and demands, parents often have to devote a great deal of time and money in accommodating new situations, such as arranging for better teachers and traveling to important events. The third phase is characterized by total commitment to the talent domain and single-minded pursuit of professional excellence. Typically, this is when the youngster has made a firm career decision, usually with the input and support of parents and teachers.

Parents may change their priorities and value perceptions of music training in response to the changing demands of musical development in the different phases. During the initial phase of exploration, parents' perceptions of musical talent and motivational characteristics may not be as important in their decisions to support music training. Some general incentives, such as developing appreciation for music or good habits, may be sufficient to sustain parents' beliefs that music training is beneficial for their children. However, when music training becomes highly demanding, as in the second phase, perceived talent and effort levels become crucial for sustained progress. Lack of motivation, talent, or both may be of concern to parents who have invested much in the process and even made many sacrifices. As children reach the point of graduation from high school, parents and students think more seriously about what career path may be more desirable and rewarding, both personally and financially. They begin to weigh the relative strengths of their children in music, academics, and other areas, as well as the potential intrinsic and extrinsic rewards associated with these domains.

PURPOSE OF THE STUDY

Musical talent development involves, and probably requires, high levels of parental support (Davidson et al., 1996). With numerous competing interests and opportunities, what motivates or influences parents' decisions to support musical talent development? How parents weigh their children's motivation, strengths, and potentialities and how parents perceive the values of music training and achievement are not well understood. Although evidence is abundant about the importance of parental support and encouragement in children's musical talent development, there has been a paucity of research on the motivational processes underlying parents' decisions and the dilemmas they may deal with in making important choices on behalf of their children.

The purpose of this study was to examine parents' expectancy and value beliefs regarding their children's music training, regular academic work, and athletic activities.

The main theoretical framework guiding this study was the expectancy-value theory of motivation (Atkinson, 1957; Parsons et al., 1983). The following research questions were addressed:

1. Do parents tend to have higher expectancy beliefs about their children's abilities and motivation in music relative to academic and athletic domains?

2. Do parents of children who have received more years of music training tend to hold higher expectancy beliefs about their children's musical competence, as well as higher aspirations for their children's achievement?

3. What are the relationships between parents' expectancy beliefs and their achievement aspirations (value) for their children?

4. Do parents experience difficulties in balancing their children's music training with academic and athletic demands, which presumably increase with age?

METHOD

Instrumentation

We developed a 44-item questionnaire to assess three aspects of parent expectancy and value beliefs in the areas of music, academics, and athletics. Similar item stems were used for each of the areas to ensure cross-domain equivalency and comparability. The three aspects of parent beliefs are as follows:

1. *parent perceptions of the child's ability and talent* (e.g., "How much natural talent do you believe that your child has in music [academics, athletics]?");

2. *parent perceptions of the effort needed to succeed and related attributes of the child and his or her motivation level* (e.g., "How much effort does it take for your child to do well in music [academics, athletics]?"; "How motivated is your child in music [academics, athletics]?"); and

3. *parent perceptions of the importance of the success in a domain* (e.g., "To what degree do you hope your child will have a career related to music [academic success, athletics]?").

To assess parents' determination or indetermination with regard to the continued development of musical talent in their children, the questionnaire also included items that indicate (a) the extent to which parents feel that the demands of music training conflict with those of academic education or athletic activities and (b) the extent to which they have difficulty deciding whether music training should give way to other more important pursuits in their children's lives.

Responses to all these items were anchored on a seven-point Likert-type scale, ranging from "low" to "high." Besides the above-mentioned constructs of interest, we elicited background information, such as whether parent(s) play an instrument, and if so, do they play professionally or not; whether they were born in the United States; and how many years the child has had music lessons.

Sample Characteristics

Participants were parents of 231 students (93 female, 137 male, 1 with missing information about gender), aged 6–18, who, at the time this survey was conducted, were attending music programs at four music institutions. We sent 400 copies of the parent questionnaire to the administration of the San Francisco Conservatory of Music (SFCM), 150 copies to the Colburn School in Los Angeles, 100 copies to the Peabody School in Baltimore, and 80 to the San Diego Youth Symphony (SDYS) for distribution among parents. A total of 94 surveys were returned from the SFCM (24%), 47 from the Colburn School (31%), 32 from the Peabody School (32%), and 58 from SDYS (73%). The first three institutions reported difficulty distributing the surveys because many parents did not come with their children for lessons. These institutions also reported difficulty recruiting some parents simply because many were not able to read English comfortably. It is likely that some of the copies sent to school administrations might not have reached the hands of parents in the distribution process, thus rendering it difficult to estimate the actual return rate. Nevertheless, the return rate for SDYS may serve as a rough estimate. We will further address the issue of return rate in our data analyses and ensuing discussion.

There was large variation in the years of music training these students reported, ranging from 0 to 12 years ($M = 5.3$, $SD = 3.3$, $Mdn = 5$). Most of their music training involved instrument playing, such as violin, viola, cello, and piano. With respect to the home environment, a majority of parents were well educated (30% of fathers and 38% of mothers reporting bachelor's degrees, and an additional 50% of fathers and 39% of mothers reporting graduate degrees). Of these parents, 55% of mothers and 40% of fathers had played musical instruments for varied periods ranging from 1 to 51 years, with a mode of 10 and 30 years, respectively. However, 13% of the parents ($n = 29$) reported that they were professional musicians. In addition, first- and second-generation immigrants were highly represented in this group of parents, presumably because of the location of the four music institutions. Forty-six percent of mothers and 40% of fathers, as well as 53% of grandparents, were born outside of the U.S. and Canada. They represented diverse origins, about half from Asia (e.g., Korea, mainland China, and Taiwan) and half from Europe and South America (e.g., Russia, Cuba, and Mexico).

Data Analyses

Data analyses reflect the exploratory nature of the current study. Factor analyses were conducted to determine the factor structure and scales of the instrument. Based on the results, subscales were formed that organized items meaningfully according to the matrix of three areas (music, academics, and athletics), and two dimensions (expectancy and value). The sample was then collapsed into four age groups for comparative analyses. Mean differences were examined by multivariate analyses of variance (MANOVA). Correlations of relevant measures were examined to explore patterns of relationships between expectancy beliefs and values within and across the three domains.

RESULTS

Factor Analyses and Scaling

First, a factor analysis was conducted with 30 items (10 items per domain; see Table 1) purportedly measuring parent beliefs about their children's competence, motivation, and value regarding the three domains. Varimax rotation yielded a seven-factor solution accounting for 68% of the variance. An inspection of factor loadings indicated that the factor structure was generally consistent with the conceptual framework; however, the within-domain competence and motivation items tended to load on the same factors. Separate factor analyses were then run with the 15 items assessing competence and motivation in the three domains and the 15 items assessing values or importance within the three domains, respectively. Except for a few items, the results were quite consistent with the conceptualization (see Table 1). To ensure the equivalency of the measures of expectancy and motivation beliefs across the three domains (music, academics, and athletics), the mean of five items with identical stems for each domain was obtained across the domains to form the measure of Competence/Motivation Belief (i.e., Expectancy), with alpha reliabilities of .78, .71, and .92, respectively (see Table 1). Likewise, the mean of five items with identical stems tapping into achievement values for each domain was obtained across domains to form the measure of Achievement Aspirations (i.e., Value) in music, academics, and athletics. The alpha reliabilities of the three measures are .79, .82, and .85, respectively (see Table 1). It should be noted that, since items with different

Table 1   Item Stems of Expectancy Beliefs and Aspirations in Music, Academics, and Athletics and Related Factor Loadings

Item Stems Applied to Music (MU), Academics (AC), Athletics (AT)	MU	AC	AT
	Factor Loadings		
Competency/Motivation			
1. How do you rate your child's skill at . . . ?	.68	.87	.91
2. How much improvement in . . . have you seen in your child?	.76	.60	.86
3. How much natural talent do you believe your child has in . . . ?	.45	.75	.86
4. How motivated is your child in . . . ?	.75	.76	.85
5. How much time does your child spend on . . . ?	.76	.25	.83
Alpha Reliability	**.78**	**.71**	**.92**
Aspirations			
6. Does achievement in . . . mean a lot in your family?	.79	.80	.88
7. To what extent are . . . activities important in your family?	.87	.81	.87
8. How important do you believe the domain is for your child?	.60	.64	.76
9. To what degree do you hope she will have a career related to . . . ?	.28	.65	.73
10. How accomplished do you expect her to be . . . as an adult?	.49	.79	.67
Alpha Reliability	**.79**	**.82**	**.85**
	Item Mean (SD)		
Effort Beliefs, Perceived Conflict, and Indecision			
How much effort does it take for your child to do well in . . . ?	4.17 (1.50)	4.01 (1.65)	4.59 (1.65)
Do you believe that effort is more important than talent for success in . . . ?	5.06 (1.40)	5.67 (1.21)	4.65 (1.46)
To what degree do the demands of music training conflict with . . . ?	(N/A)	3.71 (1.84)	3.00 (1.94)
How difficult is it, or has it been, for you to decide whether your child should continue his or her music training?	2.36 (1.74)	N/A	N/A

Note. A seven-point scale from low (1) to high (7) was used for all items.

loadings are self-weighting in forming relevant scales, items with low loadings are conceptually more peripheral than items with high loadings. Thus, the cross-domain equivalency is relative.

Preliminary Analyses

To determine whether there were systematic differences because of the apparent differential return rates among parents from the four organizations, father and mother education levels and their years of playing musical instruments were used to detect potential differences. No statistically significant difference existed among the four groups in either father or mother's education levels, as indicated by chi-square statistics. No statistically significant difference existed in years of instrument playing for either fathers or mothers. To further ascertain that no systematic difference existed between and among parents from the four institutions on the measures of Competency/Motivation Beliefs and Achievement Aspirations among students from the four musical organizations, a multivariate analysis of variance was conducted with the three Competency/Motivation Beliefs measures and the three Achievement Aspirations measures as dependent variables. No statistically significant difference was found among the four groups. Because of the comparability of samples from the four organizations, no further discrimination was made in further analyses regarding the identity of specific organizations.

Similar tests were conducted to see whether there was any difference in response as a function of the child's or the respondent's gender (mother or father). No statistically significant difference existed on the six measures of Competence/Motivation Beliefs and Achievement Aspirations. Therefore, no further distinction was made about the gender of the child and of the responding parent.

Mean Differences and Correlations as a Function of Length of Training and Age

We decided to use years of music lessons as a major grouping variable on three grounds. First, the length of formal music training is positively correlated with musical proficiency or skill level (Ericsson et al., 1990), thus indicating different levels of musical competence among these students, which, in turn, can influence parents' perceptions and decisions. Second, years of training also indicate level of commitment on the part of both parents and their child. Third, the high correlation ($r = .72$) between age and years of music lessons implies that, along with more years of training, other developmental challenges and opportunities may also emerge. After inspecting the cross-tabulation of age by years of music lessons, we divided the sample into four groups. The first group ($n = 88$) was classified as "beginners," with 0 to 3.5 years of music lessons and a mean age of 9 years ($SD = 2.92$). The second group ($n = 70$) was classified as "intermediate players," with 4 to 6.5 years of music lessons, and a mean age of 11.4 years ($SD = 2.41$). The third group ($n = 40$) was classified as "proficient players," with 7 to 9 years of music lessons and a mean age of 13.66 ($SD = 1.78$). The fourth group ($n = 33$) was classified as "advanced players," with 10 to 12 years of music lessons and a mean age of 15.87 ($SD = 1.43$). The mean differences on the measures of Competency/Motivation Beliefs and Achievement Aspirations in the three domains among the four groups are presented in Figure 1.

We conducted a MANOVA using years of music lessons (four groups) as a fixed factor, and the differences were statistically significant (Wilks' $L = .82$,

Figure I Parents' competence/motivation beliefs and achievement aspirations as a function of years of music lessons and age

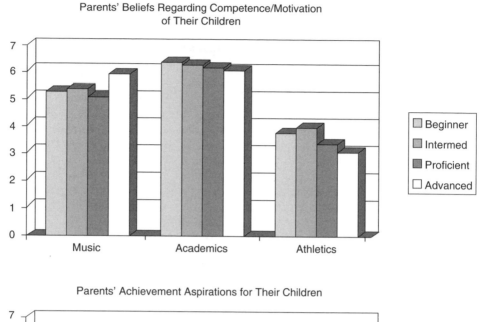

Parents' Beliefs Regarding Competence/Motivation
of Their Children

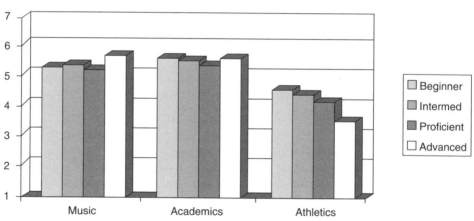

Parents' Achievement Aspirations for Their Children

$F[18, 622] = 2.59$, $p < .001$). Univariate analyses indicate statistically significant effects of years of lessons on all but the measures of competence/motivation belief and achievement aspirations in academics. Post hoc tests (Tukey HSD) showed that most differences were between the group of "advanced players" and the rest of the sample, particularly with respect to Competence/Motivation Beliefs and Achievement Aspirations in music and athletics, with parents of advanced players rating music higher and athletics lower than the rest of the sample. Together, they suggest that parents of more advanced players have higher perceptions of their children's musical competence and motivation, and hold higher aspirations for their musical achievement, but lower competence/ motivation beliefs and achievement aspirations in athletics, than parents of less advanced players. No difference was found with regard to beliefs in academics, which were high for all groups.

To determine mean differences across domains, we treated the three measures of Competency/Motivation Beliefs as a within-subject factor, while using the four groups as a between-subject factor. Wilks' Lambda for the within-subjects factor (the three measures of Competency/Motivation Beliefs) was .50 (F[2, 226] = 114.94, $p < .001$). There was also a statistically significant interaction effect of within- and between-subjects (years of music lessons) factors (Wilks' $L = .86$, F[6, 452] = 5.66, $p < .001$), suggesting that differential competence/motivation beliefs across the three domains are also a function of the length of formal music training. Likewise, Wilks' Lambda for the value factor (the three Achievement Aspirations measures) was .17 (F[2, 226] = 478.05, $p < .001$). There was also an interaction effect of within-subjects and between-subjects factors (Wilks' $L = .88$, F[6, 452] = 4.33, $p < .001$). Together, they suggest that parents differentiate their own expectancy beliefs about their children's competence and motivation in the three domains and related achievement aspirations, and such differentiation is also related to different lengths of formal music training and age.

Patterns of correlations between competence/motivation beliefs and achievement aspirations within and across the three domains further reveal effects of age and years of music training. As shown in Table 2, correlations between Competence/Motivation Beliefs and Achievement Aspirations within domains were significantly lower for beginners than the other three groups, suggesting that, with age and more years of training, parents are more likely to coordinate their aspirations with perceptions of their children's strengths and motivation. More interesting are the negative correlations between the measure of Competence/Motivation Beliefs in music and its counterpart in athletics ($r = -.26$) as well as athletic aspirations ($r = -.35$), and between Achievement Aspirations in music and its counterparts in academics ($r = -.32$) and athletics ($r = -.34$) for the group of advanced players, but not for the other three groups. These negative correlations indicate that the higher the expectancy and value beliefs in music, the lower the expectancy and value beliefs in athletic and academic areas, and vice versa. Such a correlation pattern, however, does not exist for parents of children with less than 10 years of musical lessons. Given the already small range of variations, this pattern of correlations suggests a major difference between parents of advanced players and less advanced players in their expectations and aspirations across the three domains.

Because some key items had low loadings on the factors of competence/ motivation and achievement aspirations in music, correlations of these items were inspected. The correlation between the two ability items (No. 1 and No. 3) in music was .63, and the correlation between the two career-related aspirations (No. 9 and No. 10) in music was .57. Correlations between the two ability items in music and the two career-related aspiration items range from .30 to .61, with a mean of .46, all statistically significant at the .01 level.

Table 2 Correlations of Expectancy Beliefs and Aspirations Within and Across the Three Domains by Groups of Different Skill Levels and Ages

	Comp_Music	Comp_Academics	Comp_Athletics	Aspir_Music	Aspir_Academics
Comp_Music					
Comp_Academics	.44/.34/.27/.12				
Comp_Athletics	−.06/−.03/−.20/−.26	−.04/−.03/−.12/.37			
Aspiration_Music	.49/.66/.69/.73	.20/.15/.18/−.05	.02/.04/−.01/−.17		
Aspiration_Academics	.20/.16/−.22/−.18	.34/.54/.28/.51	.25/.08/.25/.20	.23/.09/−.04/−.32	
Aspiration_Athletics	−.14/−.10/−.18/−.35	.12/.10/.08/.52	.42/.67/.78/.58	.29/.22/−.03/−.34	.30/.11/.29/.53

Note. Zero-order correlation coefficients are presented in the order of Group 1 (Beginners) to Group 4 (Advanced Players).

12

Needed Effort and Conflicts of Demands
as a Function of Length of Training and Age

If academic work is considered as important as music training, as seems to be indicated by the data, how do parents perceive the time and effort demands and potential conflict between music training, academic education, and athletics for children of different ages? To explore this issue, we ran analyses of variance with the length of music training as a factor and the six items tapping into this question as dependent variables (see Table 1 for item stems and Figure 2 for descriptive information). Statistically significant effects were found on two items. For the question "How much effort does it take for your child to do well in academic areas?," the age difference was statistically significant ($F[3, 222] = 2.69$, $p < .05$). Parents perceived that the required effort increased with age. This is also reflected in the correlation between age and this item ($r = .26$, $p < .01$). Incidentally, when the sample was broken down into three cultural groups, Asian parents tended to score higher than the rest of the sample on this item ($F[2, 226] = 6.24$, $p < .01$). For the related question "To what degree do the demands of music training and academic education conflict with each other?," the age difference was statistically significant ($F[3, 222] = 5.44$, $p < .001$). The perceived conflict apparently increases with age ($r = .34$, $p < .01$).

We further probed the possibility that how parents perceive the effort demands of a domain may be associated with their beliefs about the importance of effort for success over natural ability. We asked "Do you believe effort is more important than talent in order to be successful in music [academic subjects, athletic areas]?" Parents' responses to this question were not associated with their perceptions of effort demands. The mean responses, however, were in favor of effort ($Ms = 5.06$, 5.67, and 4.66, respectively). Given the perceived importance of effort and increasing conflicts of demands, we asked "How difficult is it, or has it been, for you to decide whether your child should continue his or her music training?" Parents' responses indicate no difficulty or ambivalence about this issue ($M = 2.36$, $SD = 1.79$). Most of them seemed quite determined in their continuing support of their children's musical development, presumably because of their strong beliefs in their children's talent potential and motivation and the parents' own values and aspirations.

DISCUSSION

The goal of this study was to examine the expectancy and value beliefs of parents whose children were attending precollege music training programs in prestigious institutions. The focus was on parental perceptions of the potential for musical development and achievement; however, competing interests and activities (mainly academics and athletics), which become increasingly prevalent during child development, were also investigated.

Results indicated that these parents saw great potential in their children in both music and academic areas, but not necessarily in athletics. Likewise,

Figure 2   Perceived effort needed to succeed, perceived conflicts between demands of music training and others, and difficulty deciding whether to continue to support children's music training

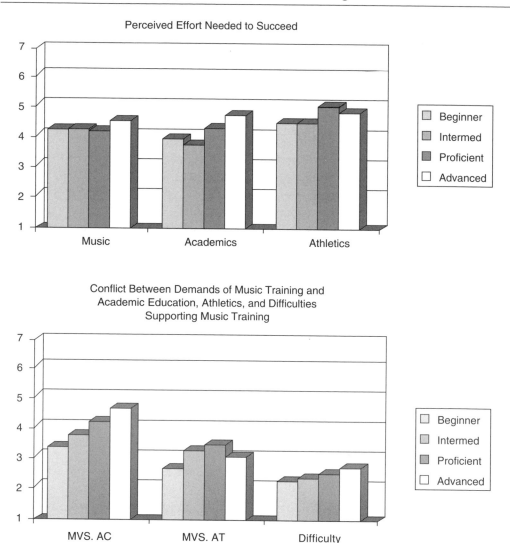

parents also value both music and academic achievement more than athletics. Given the high education levels among this group of parents, such a value orientation is not surprising. What is interesting is that parents' perceptions of the potential in their children were broadly based not only on natural talent, but also on motivational level, as items tapping into these different dimensions loaded on the same factor. It is possible that parents do not differentiate ability (or talent) and motivation (or effort level) as much as their children do (Nicholls, 1989). In their interview study, Starke, Deakin, Allard, Hodges, and Hays (1996) found that expert coaches of athletes also included motivation in their talent identification criteria. It should be noted that the two items measuring parent perceptions of ability and talent in music had relatively low loadings on the factor, but were highly correlated with each other, suggesting a certain degree of differentiation of effort/motivation and natural ability, especially in music. Although evidence in this study is not clear on the issue, how parents think of the nature of talent in music and other areas is an important question because, from an attribution point of view, innate ability is a stable, uncontrollable factor, while motivation and effort level are changeable and within the child's control. Thus, a less successful child may perceive him- or herself as lacking natural ability, whereas the parents may simply interpret it as a lack of motivation. More research is needed that incorporates both parent and child perceptions regarding talent and motivation in a systematic fashion (cf. Evans, Bickel, & Pendarvis, 2000).

A unique contribution of the present study is that, by including children of a wide range of ages and years of music lessons and looking at three important domains in school-age children's lives, different patterns of mean differences and correlations within and across domains were found between and among the four groups of different ages and lengths of music training. Although a highly homogeneous group in many regards, these parents showed interesting differences depending on their children's length of formal music training and age, consistent with the notion that, with more years of music training, parents become more single-minded in their achievement aspirations for their children. Particularly for parents of children who had received 10 to 12 years of music lessons (i.e., advanced players), higher aspirations in music were associated with lower aspirations in academic and athletic areas. These parents also showed the highest mean levels of competence/motivation beliefs and achievement aspirations in music and the lowest level in athletics. We interpret these results to indicate that parents adjust their expectations and aspirations in the single-minded support of their children's pursuits of musical development and achievement. It is likely that, while most of our "intermediate" and "proficient players" still remain in the second phase of talent development as defined by Bloom (1985), many of our "advanced players," in the transition from the second to the third phase, may be seriously considering pursuing music-related careers as they approach the end of their high school years. Changes in parents' perceptions and values may reflect the new developmental challenges and opportunities.

Regarding the relationship between expectancy beliefs and values within music, parents' perceptions of the high potential for music success (including ability and motivation) seem critical for the continuing support of their children's musical endeavors, although this relationship may be bidirectional; that is, parents with high achievement values in music tend to have biased expectancy beliefs in favor of their children. It is worth noting that this correlation tended to increase with age and more years of music lessons (see Table 2). This result seems inconsistent with the notion that parents tend to discount their child's natural ability as a determinant of success in music (Evans, Bickel, & Pendarvis, 2000; Sosniak, 1997). However, this observation should be tempered with the solutions of the factor analyses that have both ability and motivation items loading on the same factor. It should also be pointed out that achievement of eminence is not the major criterion for success in music for this group of parents as reported in a separate study that focused on the intrinsic and extrinsic aspects of motivation underlying parental support for music training (Dai & Schader, 2001).

Some limitations of the present study need to be discussed. The survey return rate was not high. Nevertheless, taking into account the small population base, the sample does represent a substantial portion of the population and is of interest in its own right. Moreover, the high education levels, high avocational interest in music, and high simultaneous emphasis on academic achievement found among these parents did not seem to be unique to this particular sample, but rather the norm for this population (Davidson et al., 1996; Evans, Bickel, & Pendarvis, 2000). Our concerns over the differential return rates and the representativeness of the sample at hand were alleviated by the comparability of parental beliefs and educational levels among parents of children from the four institutions.

Another limitation of this study is that, by breaking the sample into small groups, statistical power and interpretive confidence is decreased. How age differences and lengths of music training influence parent perceptions and values in this study also remain highly speculative given the cross-sectional nature of the data. This said, the systematic differences observed among groups are not likely to be a result of sampling error since data in this case typically err toward disguising significant effects, rather than producing artifactual differences. Thus, many observed correlations and mean differences that reach statistical significance in this study may well be underestimates of real effects because of the restricted ranges of variations and limited numbers of cases. Further research with more rigorous sampling procedures and better design (e.g., longitudinal) is needed to obtain more conclusive evidence regarding differences in parents' belief systems and value orientations and how these influence their continuing support of musical development in their children.

Despite the preliminary nature of the present investigation, with its newly developed instrument, and the exploratory nature of adopted methodologies, the results are quite promising. This study, through a lens of motivational theory, adds insights to the limited literature on the significance of parental support and involvement in the pursuit of music training. Specifically, the results of this study seem to suggest that parents may initially send their children for music training not for musical talent development per se, but for some other general value. With more advanced training and emergent challenges and opportunities, parental support for sustained engagement in music training, grounded in their expectancy beliefs and values, becomes increasingly important. Parents of children who are most musically advanced seem to regulate their perceptions and values across the three domains of importance to their children in the single-minded service of musical talent development. Thus, the view of talent development as purely an individual endeavor without the various enabling social contexts, including parental contributions, may miss an important, sometimes indispensable, component.

REFERENCES

Atkinson, J. W. (1957). Motivational determinants of risk taking behavior. *Psychological Review, 64,* 359–372.

Bloom, B. S. (Ed.). (1985). *Developing talent in young people.* New York: Ballantine Books.

Dai, D. Y., & Schader, R. M. (2001). Parents' reasons and motivations for supporting their child's music training. *Roeper Review, 24,* 23–26.

Davidson, J. W., Howe, M. J. A., Moore, D. G., & Sloboda, J. A. (1996). The role of parental influences in the development of musical performance. *British Journal of Developmental Psychology, 14,* 399–412.

Dix, T. (1993). Attributing dispositions to children: An interactional analysis of attribution in socialization. *Personality and Social Psychology Bulletin, 19,* 633–643.

Ericsson, K. A., Krampe, R., & Tesch-Romer, C. (1993). The role of deliberate practice in the acquisition of expert performance. *Psychological Review, 100,* 363–406.

Ericsson, K. A., Tesch-Romer, C., & Krampe, R. (1990). The role of practice and motivation in the acquisition of expert-level performance in real life. In M. J. A. Howe (Ed.), *Encouraging the development of exceptional skills and talents* (pp. 109–130). Leicester, England: The British Psychological Society.

Evans, R. J., Bickel, R., & Pendarvis, E. D. (2000). Musical talent: Innate or acquired? Perceptions of students, parents, and teachers. *Gifted Child Quarterly, 44,* 80–90.

Freeman, J. (1976). Developmental influences on children's perception. *Educational Research, 19,* 69–75.

Frome, P. M., & Eccles, J. S. (1998). Parents' influence on children's achievement-related perceptions. *Journal of Personality and Social Psychology, 74,* 435–452.

Gagné, F. (1999). Defining polyvalence operationally: The breadth versus depth dilemma. In N. Colangelo & S. G. Assouline (Eds.), *Talent development III: Proceedings from the 1995 Henry B. and Jocelyn Wallace National Research Symposium on Talent Development* (pp. 425–429). Scottsdale, AZ: Gifted Psychology Press.

Kemp, A. E. (1996). *The musical temperament.* Oxford, UK: Oxford University Press.

Nicholls, J. G. (1989). *The competitive ethos and democratic education.* Cambridge, MA: Harvard University Press.

Parsons, J. E., Adler, T. F., Futterman, R., Goff, S. B., Kaczala, C. M., Meece, J. L., & Midgley, C. (1983). Expectancies, values, and academic behaviors. In J. T. Spence (Ed.), *Achievement and achievement motivation* (pp. 75–146). San Francisco: Freeman.

Parsons, J. E., Adler, T. F., & Kaczala, C. M. (1982). Socialization of achievement attitudes and beliefs: Parental influences. *Child Development, 53,* 310–321.

Philips, D. (1987). Socialization of perceived academic competence among highly competent children. *Child Development, 58,* 1308–1320.

Sloboda, J. A., Davidson, J. W., Howe, M. J. A., & Moore, D. G. (1996). The role of practice in the development of performing musicians. *British Journal of Psychology, 87,* 287–309.

Sosniak, L. A. (1997). The tortoise, the hare, and the development of talent. In N. Colangelo & G. A. Davis (Eds.), *Handbook of gifted education* (2nd ed., pp. 207–217). Boston: Allyn and Bacon.

Starke, J. L., Deakin, J. M., Allard, F., Hodges, N. J., & Hayes, A. (1996). Deliberate practice in sports: What is it anyway? In K. A. Ericsson (Ed.), *The road to excellence: The acquisition of expert performance in the arts and sciences, sports, and games* (pp. 81–106). Mahwah, NJ: Erlbaum.

2

Musical Talent: Innate or Acquired? Perceptions of Students, Parents, and Teachers

Robert J. Evans

Robert Bickel

Edwina D. Pendarvis

Marshall University

Secondary analysis of descriptive data concerning musically gifted students, their parents, and their teachers yields distinctive attribution patterns for each group. The patterns describe this group of students as attributing much of their success to inborn ability and hard work. These accomplished students, however, describe family members and friends as

---

Editor's Note: From Evans, R. J., Bickel, R., & Pendarvis, E. D. (2000). Musical talent: Innate or acquired? Perceptions of students, parents, and teachers. *Gifted Child Quarterly*, *44*(2), 80-90. © 2000 National Association for Gifted Children. Reprinted with permission.

discouraging their musical development. Parents, in sharp contrast, report their children as having only ordinary levels of inborn talent, and they attribute their children's musical accomplishments to encouragement provided by family and friends. Teachers in this study attribute students' musical development to innate talent, hard work, and schooling. Differences among these attribution patterns are surprising, but are consistent with research that suggests that individuals often make causal attributions that are self-serving giving a good deal of credit to their own characteristics or influence.

The controversy over *The Bell Curve* (Herrnstein & Murray, 1994) was acrimonious and sustained. Reviews, articles, and monographs published in support or repudiation of Herrnstein and Murray's IQ-intensive genetic determinism demonstrated continued interest in the issue of nature versus nurture as influences on human performance (see, for example, Kinchloe, Steinberg, & Gresson, 1996). Herrnstein and Murray's claims notwithstanding, decades of research have not resolved this issue and, in fact, may never resolve it (Berliner & Biddle, 1995).

Nevertheless, a related, nontrivial question that can be answered is which source is thought to influence achievement more: environmental circumstances or inherited ability? The research reported herein attempts to describe the nature versus nurture accounts of musically gifted students, their parents, and their teachers. Specifically, we attempt to determine whether musically talented students attribute their attainments primarily to inborn talent or to external factors, such as formal education, parental support, and other environmental influences. We also investigate whether the parents and teachers of these musically accomplished young people respond with similar or different attribution patterns to the nature versus nurture issue.

Putting the Research to Use

Due to postulated connections between people's beliefs and their actions, this type of research, focusing on gifted students, may lead to a better understanding of patterns of attributional thinking that promote outstanding accomplishments. Such an understanding could lead to development of instructional or counseling methods that encourage productive attributional patterns. It seems reasonable, too, that productive patterns may vary from one group to another. It may be good for children to regard themselves as innately talented, as did the children in our group. However, if parents saw innate talent as the singular factor in their children's accomplishments—if they failed to see their efforts on behalf of their children's achievement as perhaps the most significant factor in their children's achievement—they might not put forth much effort. A productive attributional pattern for teachers of gifted children might be another explanatory pattern altogether. Our group of teachers had high opinions of their students' ability, *and* they regarded formal instruction as an important contributor to their accomplishments. Perhaps the "Pygmalion effect" contributed to these children's accomplishments. Research studies suggest that high expectations by teachers has a positive effect on children's achievement.

Our research on gifted children's, their parents', and their teachers' patterns of perception is not intended to deny the importance of continuing research designed to discover, in as objective terms as possible, the relative contributions of heredity and environment to outstanding accomplishment. It simply suggest that perceptions regarding the nature/nurture dichotomy may be relevant to educators and counselors who seek to understand gifted children and promote talent development.

LITERATURE REVIEW

Attributional theory, deriving in large part from the work of Rotter (1954) and Heider (1958), posits the existence of a relationship between peoples' perceptions of the sources of their success or failure and their actual performance. Attributional research suggests that different groups account for their performance in predictably different ways (Collier, 1994). Much of this work reports that high achievers tend to take credit for their accomplishments in terms of their own ability and effort (Antaki, 1994).

Underachievers' attribution patterns are more complex, and tend to be self-defeating (Graham, 1990). Underachievers often attribute their failures to either their own lack of innate ability or to external factors, such as the difficulty of the task. Even more interesting for present purposes, underachievers typically attribute their occasional successes to external factors. These include circumstances such as the easiness of the task, teacher bias in their favor, and even luck. In discussing attribution patterns, however, it is important to bear in mind that attributions and expectations may be inconsistent with independent measures of students' traits (Marsh, 1984; Peterson & Barrett, 1987). Battle (1972), for example, compared students with above-average IQ scores and below-average IQ scores with regard to expectations of academic success. Battle found that above-average students who did not expect to do well in academic subjects performed at a lower level than below-average students who expected to succeed.

Apparently, ability and expectations have independent effects. Whatever students' measured ability, their performance may be enhanced or undercut depending on their expectations and the way they account for their own success or failure (Peterson & Barrett, 1987; Velez, 1989).

According to Licht and Dweck (1984), this process can be a major contributor to undcrachievement because "to conclude that one does not have the ability to do well implies that an escalation of effort would be fruitless" (p. 628). Achievement level, as a result, depends in part on students' understanding of their control over events and outcomes in their own lives (Kelly, 1993).

Research has not yet determined if artistically gifted students are like the high academic achievers studied by Marsh (1984) and Antaki (1994), who attribute their success to internal factors rather than external ones. It is important to bear in mind, however, that perceptions of the causes of high and low levels of achievement depend in part on social position. Children from low-socioeconomic-status families tend to have an external locus of control (Rotter, 1972), while high-socioeconomic-status students tend to explain their behavior in internal terms, such as high academic ability or ability to work hard (Brantlinger, 1993). Since being identified as gifted is also positively associated with socioeconomic status, it is likely that artistically gifted students will also have an internal locus of control. If so, we would expect them to attribute their success, in large part, to their own talent or at least their capacity for hard work.

Gifted students' explanations of their success also may be influenced by their parents' beliefs and by dominant social expectations. In the U.S., giftedness traditionally has been regarded as substantially inborn (see, for example, Friedman & Rogers, 1998; Hollingworth, 1942; Terman, 1925). As a result, gifted children, as well as their parents, are influenced to account for their high achievement by reference to inborn ability.

It is true that Cox, Daniel, and Boston (1985), reported that MacArthur fellows, a highly talented group that includes writers, filmmakers, and musicians, attributed their achievement to extraordinary support from their parents. This remains, however, an uncommon exception to the usual focus on innate ability. The belief in inborn ability is so common-place in the U.S. that few studies have focused on the family and school as critical factors in the development of exceptional talent. Bloom (1985), however, followed the precedent set by Pressey (1955) in studying the influence of family and school factors in precocious development. Bloom's work, reported in *Developing Talent in Young People*, emphasized environmental factors and found little evidence of extraordinary early musical talent among a group of world-class musicians.

An important part of Bloom's talent development research project was Sosniak's (1985) retrospective study of 21 unusually accomplished pianists. Sosniak found that these world-class pianists manifested several common characteristics. Among the demographic traits were membership in families of relatively high socioeconomic status. In addition, all were White, and most were male. Sosniak concluded that these pianists' accomplishments could not have been predicted based on early identification of talent. Parents of Sosniak's musically gifted subjects did not provide reports that clearly distinguished the talent of this group from their less-accomplished siblings. Nevertheless, in spite of the absence of supporting evidence, parents had unusually high expectations for the accomplished group and were convinced that they were, in fact, gifted.

According to Sosniak, parents' beliefs as to their children's musical talent may have hastened the start and accelerated the pace of musical instruction. Teachers reported that these same accomplished young pianists learned rapidly, however. In addition, they responded quickly and effectively to suggestions for improvement. Sosniak's study does not include a direct investigation of causal attributions. Her research makes clear, however, that objective accounts of students' early performance and reports of extraordinary musical instruction and experience did not point to inborn giftedness.

METHODS

The many studies of attributions that students make about causal relations between internal or external factors in order to explain outstanding achievement and Sosniak's study of musically accomplished youngsters, with its obvious implications for our interest in attributional patterns, led us to investigate perceptions of ability and other advantages in a group of musically talented students. These same factors prompted us to compare students' attributions regarding the source of their accomplishments with their parents' and teachers' attribution patterns.

Subjects

The Blue Lake Fine Arts Camp (BLFAC), the site of this study, is typical of many fine arts programs. The students who attended the 1996 BLFAC International Program in Twin Lakes, Mich., were initially accepted into the BLFAC summer program based upon music teacher and school administrator recommendations. From the summer program consisting of nearly 4,000 students, those identified as the most accomplished were invited to audition for the prestigious International Program. Only 260, or 7%, were chosen to participate. Given the highly selective character of the International Program, we identified its participants as musically gifted. International Program participants ranged in age from 12 to 17. Eighty-three were in the orchestra, 85 in the symphonic band, 84 in the choir, and 16 in the jazz band. Nearly 80% of the participants were White, with small numbers of Blacks, Hispanics, Native Americans, and Asians. Almost all came from households with annual incomes over $60,000. Their parents owned their own homes, and graduate degrees were commonplace, as was employment in professional occupations. In short, these musically gifted students had the ethnic and class characteristics we could expect. Much as with other students identified as gifted or unusually capable, they were overwhelmingly native Whites, and, with rare exceptions, came from families marked by high levels of education, income, and occupational attainment (Brantlinger, 1993; Sosniak, 1985; Tyler-Wood & Carri, 1993; Velez, 1989).

These students had, moreover, received favorable attention from school teachers and administrators. This accounted for their acceptance at the Blue Lake Fine Arts Camp and for the opportunity to compete for a position in the highly selective International Program. Favorable attention from school personnel is much more common among socially and economically advantaged students than among others (Howley, Howley, & Pendarvis, 1995; Kelly, 1993; Lareau, 1989; Oakes, 1986; Swartz, 1997).

Data Collection

During spring and summer pre-European tour rehearsals, survey packets including the questionnaires described below were mailed to each of the 260 International Program participants. Mailing was scheduled so that participants received the packets during the break between a May weekend rehearsal and the intensive rehearsal week in June. Each packet contained a cover letter with instructions, a questionnaire for the student participant, a questionnaire for his or her parents, and a questionnaire for the teacher who initially recommended the student for BLFAC. The packets also contained self-addressed stamped envelopes to return completed surveys directly to us by mail.

Instrument

Twenty-one items were common to each of the questionnaires, with minor variations in wording to reflect respondents' role as student, parent, or teacher. Some of the information to be collected was attitudinal, and some was prosaically factual. Each of the questions on each questionnaire was a Likert item, with a fixed set of five response categories determined by the nature of the question (student questions are listed in Table 1).

Unfortunately, conception and execution of this data collection effort preceded development of our interest in attribution patterns for giftedness. Consequently, the questionnaires were not designed for scale development. Instead, they were intended to elicit diffusely descriptive information for a preliminary report on a broad range of characteristics of an unusually capable subset of students involved in a summer camp for musically accomplished students, as well as their parents and teachers.

Mode of Analysis

For this paper, as a result of this change in plans, we performed a secondary analysis. We are not using the information in the questionnaires for rather loosely defined descriptive purposes as originally planned. Instead, we employed

Table I   Opportunities for Attribution: Items With Interpretable Loadings

- I believe I was born with special musical abilities.
- I believe my teachers feel I was born with special musical abilities.
- I believe my friends feel I was born with special musical abilities.
- At what age did you first become interested in singing or playing?
- At what age did you first sing or play for family, friends, or others?
- Did close friends support your musical interests?
- Did family members support your musical interests?
- Were preschool teachers supportive of your musical interests?
- Were regular school teachers supportive of your musical interests?
- How old were you when you received your first special award or recognition in school?
- How many years have you studied music in school?
- How many years have you taken private lessons?
- Did you want to practice?

Note. Items are taken from the Student Questionnaire. The same items, with minor changes in wording depending on the role of the respondent, appear on Teacher and Parent Questionnaires. All items have five fixed response categories. The kinds of categories depend on the substance of the question.

selected questionnaire items in what amounts to an opportunistic effort to identify factors that students, parents, and teachers use in explaining students' musical development. In effect, we were trying to discern attributions used in accounting for musical development and looking for distinctive patterns of attribution among the three sets of respondents.

The hoped-for outcome was a set of ideal-types or epitomes that succinctly characterize students, parents, and teachers in terms of how they account for students' musical attainments. We were especially interested in identifying similarities and differences in ideal-typical attribution patterns among the three groups.

It was not our intention to collect data that would constitute a probability sample. Instead, we mailed questionnaires to all members of the three populations of prospective respondents: students, their parents, and their teachers. Thus, the populations consisted of 260 accomplished student musicians, 260 sets of parents, and 260 teachers.

In this secondary analysis, however, our interest was no longer limited to these populations. While acknowledging strict limitations on selection of prospective respondents, we hope tentatively to offer an analysis of broader interest, even though generalizability is obviously problematic.

We acknowledge, of course, that there is no sound statistical basis for such inferences. Nevertheless, as we have already noted, the students in our sample are, in a variety of readily observable ways, much like gifted students reported by many other observers. They are mainly native-born Whites from comparatively high-socioeconomic-status families. As with other kinds of giftedness, being unusually accomplished musically rarely provides a means of dramatic upward social mobility for young people. Instead, students with such attributes are usually those born into ethnically, socially, and economically advantaged circumstances.

The gifted students we studied, their families of origin, their teachers, and their pertinent in-school and out-of-school experiences are socially typical of those we would expect to find associated with a highly selective program for unusually capable young people.

Response Rate

The response rate, with two waves of the mail-out questionnaires, was 48% for students, 47% for parents, and 34% for teachers. This translates into 125 student respondents, 123 parent respondents, and 88 teacher respondents. The relatively low return rates make both internal and external validity problematic, which we discuss below.

Data Analysis

The statistical tool used to analyze the questionnaire data for each category of respondents was alpha factor analysis. It was our intention to collect and analyze population data for each of the three groups, producing a conceptually parsimonious summary of student, parent, and teacher attribution patterns. This objective seemed well-suited to use of alpha factor analysis (Nunnally & Bernstein, 1994; Tacq, 1997). In this vein, it is useful to recall that, in the first edition of Nunnally's now-classic text *Psychometric Theory*, he admonished factor analysts that misinterpretation is especially likely with analyses having fewer than 10 subjects per interpreted item (Nunnally, 1967). This is a criterion that we nearly meet for two groups, students and parents, but not for teachers. In our analyses, the number of subjects per item is approximately 9.6 for students and 9.5 for parents, but only 6.8 for teachers. More recently, Grimm and Yarnold (1995) have suggested that factor analyses with as few as five respondents per item are acceptable, provided the total number of respondents is at least 100. The student and parent groups easily meet these criteria, but there are only 88 teachers. Tabachnik and Fidell (1996) have still another rule of thumb: At least 300 cases are needed, unless each factor has loadings of .800 or more. If the latter criterion is met, 150 cases will do.

Stevens (1996), however, has advised avoiding fixed respondents-per-item and total-sample criteria through use of a straightforward means of tying the interpretability of factor loadings to sample size. Specifically, Stevens recommended that factor analysts forego the usual rule of thumb, whereby they retain for interpretation loadings of .300 or greater. In place of this convention, Stevens provided simple but explicit guidelines for increasing the numerical magnitude of interpreted loadings as sample size decreases. Loadings that fall below this value are not interpreted. It is true that our ratio of respondents to items is, by most standards, not large. In view of this, we have followed Stevens' procedure, interpreting only factor loadings with absolute values of .463 or higher for students, .471 or higher for parents, and .548 or higher for teachers (also see Nunnally & Bernstein, 1994).

As a result, the number of items with loadings that are actually reported drops to 13. (See Tables 3, 4, and 5.) The remaining nine items are not included for interpretation.

Interpretable Factors

Scree plots for each of the three groups of respondents appear in Figure 1. The break in the plots for students and teachers clearly occurs after the second factor has been extracted. The break in the parent plot is less obvious and illustrates the often judgment-call way in which scree plots must be interpreted. In this instance, the break seems to occur after the third factor has been extracted. Accordingly, usual rules of thumb for scree plots would have us retain for interpretation the first two factors for students and teachers and the first three for parents (Johnson & Wichern, 1998).

Furthermore, for the parent group, each of the three factors has at least three interpretably large loadings. For students, however, the third component had only one interpretably large loading, and for teachers there were none. For each of the seven retained factors, moreover, the interpretable loadings have moderate to high levels of internal consistency, with values of Cronbach's alpha ranging from .61 to .81 (Frary, 1995; Paita, Love, Leftwachra, & Grabovsky, 1999). Consistent with the Kaiser criterion for interpretability, each of the retained factors has an eigenvalue above 1.00 (Grimm & Yarnold, 1995), and each factor explains more than 10% of the total variance in the data set. For each of the three groups, moreover, none of the variables has a loading large enough to be interpretable on more than one factor. In each group, while each factor has at least two interpretably large loadings, none has more than five. For each group, each factor has one or more loadings that is very close to zero. Finally, Table 2 makes clear that the correlations among the obliquely rotated factors for each group are not strong. In short, Thurstone's simple structure is usefully approximated for each set of respondents (Nunnally & Bernstein, 1994; Tabachnik & Fidell 1996). Thus, retention of three factors for interpretation for the parent group and two factors for the student and teacher groups seems a reasonable decision, defensible on a variety of statistical grounds (Grimm & Yarnold, 1995; Tacq, 1997).

Rotation of Factors

The choice of a method of rotation to increase interpretability of factors often seems essentially arbitrary (Pedhazur & Schmelkin, 1991). When deciding whether to use orthogonal or oblique rotation, however, substantive criteria should be employed (SAS Institute, 1990; Tacq, 1997). Specifically, do we expect the variables we are using to yield factors reflecting constructs that correspond to everyday phenomena that are, in fact, independent or associated? In the present instance, the past 30 years of research in education and related areas

Figure 1   Scree Plots: Students, Parents and Teachers

Scree Plot: Students
Eigenvalues Through Break in Plot

```
2.771              *

2.312                    *

1.380                          *
1.270                                *
1.032                                      *
          1     2     3     4     5
```

Scree Plot:Parents
Eigenvalues Through Break in Plot

```
3.278              *

2.218                    *

1.634                          *
1.056                                *
 .978                                      *
          1     2     3     4     5
```

Scree Plot: Teachers
Eigenvalues Through Break in Plot

```
3.182              *

2.416                    *

1.436                          *
1.253                                *
1.055                                      *
          1     2     3     4     5
```

makes it virtually certain that individual, family, school, and a variety of contextual factors will be associated (see, for example, Bryk & Raudenbush, 1992; Coleman et al., 1966; Farkas, 1996; Iversen, 1991; Lareau, 1989). Each of these sets of variables constitutes part of a context of interrelated, mutually implicative social and cultural influences. Consequently, we have concluded that orthogonal rotation is inconsistent with substantive knowledge pertinent to our research, and we employ oblique rotation. The specific rotation method is direct Oblimin, the only oblique rotation procedure available with our SPSS software.

Oblique rotation produces two matrices: the pattern matrix and the structure matrix. The two matrices are identical only if the factors are, in fact, orthogonal. Otherwise, the pattern matrix, with loadings analogous to partial standardized regression coefficients, is the one interpreted (Stevens, 1996; Tabachnik & Fidell, 1996). Pattern matrices are reported and interpreted in this

Table 2   Rationale for Oblique Rotation

Students: Factor Correlation Matrix

	I	II
I		
II	−.032	

Parents: Factor Correlation Matrix

	I	II	III
I			
II	.183		
III	.151	−.046	

Teachers: Factor Correlation Matrix

	I	II
I		
II	−.130	

paper. Component correlation matrices following oblique rotation appear in Table 2. As noted above, there are modest correlations among some factors, indicating that they are, in fact, not orthogonal.

RESULTS

The basic question that undergirds our work can be simply stated: Do students, parents, and teachers account for students' musical success in the same ways? If so, the factor structures for all three groups will be the same. If not, different factor structures, representing differing patterns of attribution, will emerge, which will permit construction of distinctive ideal-types, epitomizing the attribution patterns for each of the three groups.

Role-Specific Attributions: Students

The two factors used in interpreting students' role-specific attributions are reported in Table 3. The first factor (named *Talent Discouraged*) has three interpretable loadings that refer to innate musical ability and two that refer to support for musical development provided by parents and friends.

Clearly, students are convinced that they have innate musical talent. Moreover, they view their teachers and friends as emphatically sharing this judgment. Students' talent and the shared belief as to its existence and value are credited by students with fostering their musical development.

But, note the two negative loadings corresponding to encouragement offered by family and friends. These same students saw family and friends as actively discouraging their musical development. The interpretable loadings on

Table 3   Students' Role-Specific Attributions of Musical
                Development: Mavericks*

	Talent Discouraged	Profitable Involvement
Shared Belief in Talent Fostered Musical Development		
Students Believe	.679	−.068
Teachers Believe	.662	−.030
Friends Believe	.730	.035
Early Involvement Fostered Musical Development		
Early Interest	.073	.499
Early Performance	−.095	.676
Social Support Fostered Musical Development		
Friends Encourage	−.489	.052
Family Encourages	−.529	−.022
School Support Fostered Musical Development		
Preschool Teachers	−.370	−.253
School Teachers	−.114	.001
In-School Recognition	−.071	.487
Work Fostered Musical Development		
Years of School Work	.030	.664
Years of Private Work	.000	.465
Prone to Practice	−.114	−.001
Cronbach's Alpha	.76	.68
Eigenvalues	2.771	2.312
Variance Explained	21.3%	17.8%
Total = 39.1%		
n = 125		

Note. Bartlett Test of Sphericity = 375.71, $p < .00001$; Kaiser-Meyer-Olkin Test of Sampling
Adequacy = .6311; *Loadings less than .463 not interpreted.

the second student factor (named *Profitable Involvement*), however, indicate that
in spite of students' judgment that family and friends discouraged their musical development, the students experienced early exposure and involvement in
music, worked long and hard on their musical growth both in and out of school,
and received in-school recognition for their accomplishments.

Role-Specific Attributions: Parents

Parents' attribution patterns are sharply different from students' patterns.
The first three interpretable loadings on the first parent factor (named *No-Talent*

Table 4   Parents' Role-Specific Attributions of Musical Development: Plodders*

	I No-Talent Impediment	II Encouraged Commitment	III Payoff-Denied Frustration
Shared Belief in Talent Fostered Musical Development			
Student Believes	−.603	−.127	−.026
Teachers Believe	−.793	−.151	−.121
Friends Believe	−.797	−.283	−.162
Early Exposure Fostered Musical Development			
Early Interest	−.379	.332	−.307
Early Performance	.384	.802	.242
Social Support Fostered Musical Development			
Friends Encourage	.403	.516	.044
Family Encourages	.387	.497	.242
School Support Fostered Musical Development			
Preschool Teachers	.376	.280	.189
School Teachers	.366	.344	−.106
In-School Recognition	.084	.301	−.479
Work Fostered Musical Development			
Years of School Work	−.206	.043	−.620
Years of Private Work	−.097	−.150	−.817
Prone to Practice	.154	.442	.057
Cronbach's Alpha	.81	.61	.75
Eigenvalues	3.278	2.218	1.634
Variance Explained	25.2%	17.1%	12.6%

Total = 54.8%
n = 123

Note. Bartlett Test of Sphericity = 462.097, $p < .00001$; Kaiser-Meyer-Olkin Test of Sampling Adequacy = .671; *Loadings less than .471 not interpreted.

Impediment) in Table 4 make clear that parents' views do not correspond to the students' judgment that their musical success can be attributed to a shared belief in their innate talent. On the contrary, these three negative loadings make evident that parents are convinced that no one attributes musical ability to students. Instead, we see an attribution pattern that suggests an absence of belief in students' talent.

The magnitude and consistency of the negative loadings is striking, especially when contrasted with student attributions and, as we shall see, with teacher attributions. The parents' loadings suggest that they believe and that they attribute to others the belief that students' lack of talent serves as an important impediment to their musical development. In addition, although students' *Profitable Involvement* factor showed an early interest in music, parents attribute not merely a lack of early interest, but an early aversion to music. This seems a reasonable interpretation of the negative loading corresponding to the *Early Interest* variable in the *No-Talent Impediment factor*.

Furthermore, much of the high level of contrast between students and parents pertains to payoffs from hard work. The third factor (named *Payoff-Denied Frustration*) in parents' attribution pattern suggests that hard work leads not merely to disappointment, but may be so frustrating as to be self-defeating. The accompanying absence of in-school recognition seems reasonably interpreted as further undercutting students' musical development. In spite of the lack of both talent and early musical interest that parents attribute to students, the second factor (named *Encouraged Commitment*) indicates that early exposure and involvement, coupled with encouragement offered by friends and family, along with students' predisposition to work, account for students' musical development. This holds, according to parents, in spite of the purportedly dis-appointing, even perniciously frustrating, influence of hard work itself.

Were it not for the positive loading corresponding to the *Prone to Practice* variable, the negative loadings for in-school and out-of-school work might very well be interpreted to mean that parents judge students' failure to work as diminishing their musical development. In the overall context of factors and loadings found here, however, the negative loadings on the work variables seem better viewed as measures of frustration and lack of payoff. This is the sort of thing one might expect for students who are judged by all to lack musical talent, but who are still actively engaged in music.

It is important to remember, however, that if students had not been identified as musically accomplished, they would not be represented in this data set. According to parents, these accomplishments—even an appearance of giftedness—are due largely to the encouragement offered by family and friends in support of students in their against-the-odds commitment to musical development.

Role-Specific Attributions: Teachers

Teachers' attribution patterns, as manifest in the factors reported in Table 5, are very similar to those of students. As with students themselves, and in dra-matic contrast to the parent group, teachers attribute students' musical devel-opment, at least in good part, to shared recognition of students' musical talent. This is abundantly evident in the second factor for teachers (named simply *Talent*). Teachers' first factor (for which we borrow the name *Profitable Involvement* from students' pattern of attributions) also shows that they attribute students' musical development to payoffs from hard work, both in and out of school, and to in-school recognition, much as do students. This contrasts sharply with parents' patterns of attribution.

Teachers' second factor (*Talent*) is much like students' first, attributing students' musical attainments to innate talent. Unlike students, however, teachers do not judge that family and friends have discouraged (or encouraged)

Table 5 Teachers' Role-Specific Attributions of Musical Development: Self-Starters*

	Profitable Involvement	Talent
Shared Belief in Talent Fostered Musical Development		
Student Believes	.061	.878
Teachers Believe	−.028	.569
Friends Believe	−.031	.790
Early Exposure Fostered Musical Development		
Early Interest	.618	.072
Early Performance	.619	−.141
School Support Fostered Musical Development		
Friends Encourage	.414	−.453
Family Encourages	.354	−.377
Social Support Fostered Musical Development		
Preschool Teachers	.342	−.174
School Teachers	.121	−.097
In-School Recognition	.789	−.086
Work Fostered Musical Development		
Years of School Work	.701	−.087
Years of Private Work	.555	.026
Prone to Practice	−.101	−.106
Cronbach's Alpha	.78	.81
Eigenvalues	3.182	2.416
Variance Explained	24.5%	18.6%

Total = 43.1%
n = 88

Note. Bartlett Test of Sphericity = 283.655, $p < .00001$; Kaiser-Meyer-Olkin Test of Sampling Adequacy = .590; *Loadings less than .548 not interpreted.

students' musical development. Again, this is very different from parents' view. All told, results for teachers and students are quite similar, while parents differ sharply from both.

Ideal Types

By way of further interpreting the attribution patterns manifest in the factors, we will construct three ideal-types, epitomes of these musically accomplished students, according to accounts derived from responses of students, parents, and teachers.

Maverick. The ideal-type constructed according to students' attributions is one we will call a profitably involved, talented maverick. Innate musical ability, beneficial schooling, and fruitful hard work are of paramount importance. Although early exposure and involvement in musical activity were helpful, student success was achieved in spite of the discouraging influences of family and friends. Students see themselves as being able, determined, and well-served by schooling and work as they continue to invest time and effort in their musical growth. They do this in spite of the opposition they attribute to family and friends. It is this confluence of attributions that earns students' pattern the "maverick" characterization.

Self-starter. The primary differences between students and teachers is in the teacher group's absence of interpretable loadings with respect to support supplied by family and friends. Whereas students attribute a discouraging influence to those nominally closest to them, teachers see no such influence. As with students themselves, teachers' attributions portray students as profitably involved, talented, and school-backed. However, they find neither interest in, nor opposition to, this process among family and friends. This confluence of attributions prompts the "self-starter" characterization for the teachers' pattern.

Plodder. The ideal-type constructed for parents is sharply at odds with that of both students and teachers. The impeding of students' musical development because of a lack of talent and lack of early interest, coupled with the frustrations born of hard work that does not pay off, in the presence of ongoing encouragement and student commitment, earns the "plodder" characterization. Ordinary in talent and poorly served by both school-based and private investments of time and energy, the plodder continues with his or her musical development. In the absence of exceptional talent, the frustrations seem inevitable and substantial, and ongoing musical development may come as a surprise for which the price was too high. The encouragement and early musical involvement fostered by family and friends must be judged to be powerful forces, indeed, for the "plodder" to continue, actually gaining musical capability over time.

DISCUSSION

We have made a determined effort to identify the methodological deficiencies in the research reported above. The sample size is not large in relation to the number of items on each questionnaire, and return rates are lower than we would have liked. Using now-familiar terminology introduced by Campbell and Stanley (1963), internal validity and external validity may be problematic because of the related problems of sample size and return rate.

Our foregoing discussion addressed the problem of internal validity, making the case that the number of respondents per item in each factor is sufficiently large so that interpretations are justifiable. Moreover, there is nothing strained or tendentious about the interpretation we have given to our factor analysis results. We have proceeded in a cautiously exploratory manner, and the factors seem usefully, even if tentatively, interpretable as ideal-typical response patterns, distinctively epitomizing the attributions of the three groups. External validity, however, remains problematic. The response rate for the three groups varies from 48% for students to 47% for parents to 34% for teachers. The possibility that our data set yields atypical results when applied to the three populations of respondents is quite real, even though we attempted to collect population data, rather than a probability sample. It is useful to recognize, however, that the three groups are approximately homogeneous internally with regard to variables that may be confounded with attribution patterns, such as education, occupation, income, and ethnicity. Although the statistical basis for generalizability is uncertain due to the possibility of important variables being confounded with returns, the internal homogeneity of our three groups makes this much less likely than would typically be the case.

In the same vein, it bears repeating that the students in our sample are, in socially consequential ways, much like the gifted students reported by many other observers. They are mainly native-born Whites of comparatively high socioeconomic status. As with other kinds of giftedness, being unusually accomplished musically rarely provides a means of dramatic upward social mobility. Instead, students with these accomplishments are usually those born into ethnically, socially, and economically advantaged circumstances. These are, moreover, the students whose giftedness is most likely to be recognized, nurtured, and rewarded by teachers and others. Perhaps the strongest claim we can make on behalf of our analysis and interpretation is that they make clear-cut sense. *Maverick, Self-Starter,* and *Plodder* are, to be sure, nothing more nor less than informed interpretations of statistical analyses. Nevertheless, they do make dramatically evident the striking differences between students' and teachers' attributions, on the one hand, and parents' attributions, on the other.

Conclusions

At the outset, we asked if musically accomplished students were much like other high achievers, attributing their talent, in good part, to innate ability. It is obvious that analysis of our data leads us to an emphatic "Yes."

It is also true, however, that attribution patterns are complex, and their comparisons yield surprises. There is nothing in the literature on giftedness that would have prepared us for the finding that musically accomplished students perceive family and friends as discouraging their efforts at musical development.

Similarly, there is nothing in the literature on giftedness that would have prepared us for the finding that parents of musically accomplished students would have a wildly contradictory view, judging students' success to have occurred because of encouragement and experience and in spite of a lack of innate ability. Based on the literature on giftedness, we would have expected to find the opposite. The attribution pattern of teachers, in fact, approximates those we would expect to find for parents, since it includes innate ability, interest, exposure and involvement, and hard work. Even teachers' attribution pattern, however, does not include encouragement by family and friends. This research sensitizes us to the possibility that attribution patterns concerning giftedness may be activity-specific, varying from one endeavor to another. Too facile a generalization from one set of activities to another may generate confusion and misunderstanding. Certainly, attribution patterns pertaining to students specifically gifted in music are, in some ways, quite different from numerous reports concerning students in other categories of giftedness.

In spite of these surprises, however, there is a common characteristic in all of our patterns. All the patterns are consistent with Marsh's (1984) finding that attributions of sources of accomplishment tend to be self-serving. Parents in our study seem to regard their own contributions of encouragement and opportunities for involvement in music as crucial to their children's accomplishments—far more crucial than inborn ability. The teachers seem to regard the schoolwork and in-school rewards as important influences in the development of talented children's musical ability; they tended to discount the influence of family and friends. The students themselves regarded their own ability and hard work as important sources of their success.

This descriptive study suggests the complexity of attributional responses. The differences in perception between students, teachers, and parents make a case for further research identifying various groups' perceptions of the sources of high achievement. The research-documented interactions between students' perceptions about the causes of high achievement and their actual levels of performance may be only a part of the phenomenon of superior accomplishment. How parents feel about the reasons their children achieve and how teachers feel about why their students achieve may also be important contributors to gifted children's levels of achievement.

REFERENCES

Antaki, C. (1994). *Explaining and arguing: The social organization of accounts*. London: Sage.

Battle, E. (1972). Motivational determinants of academic competence. In J. Rotter, J. Chance, & E. Phares (Eds.), *Applications of a social learning theory of personality* (pp. 155–168). New York: Holt, Rinehart, and Winston.

Berliner, D., & Biddle, B. (1995). *The manufactured crisis*. Reading, MA: Addison-Wesley.

Bloom, B. (1985). *Developing talent in young people*. New York: The Free Press.

Brantlinger, J. (1993). *The politics of social class in secondary school*. New York: Teachers College Press.

Bryk, A., & Raudenbush, S. (1992). *Hierarchical linear modeling*. Newbury Park, CA: Sage.

Campbell, D., & Stanley, J, (1963). Experimental and quasi-experimental designs for research on teaching. In N. Gage (Ed.), *Handbook of research on teaching* (pp. 171–246). Chicago: Rand McNally.

Coleman, J., Campbell, E., Hobson, C., McPartland, J., Mood, A., Weinfeld, F., & York, R. (1966). *Equality of educational opportunity*. Washington, DC: U.S. Government Printing Office.

Collier, G. (1994). *Social origins of mental ability*. New York: John Wiley.

Cox, J., Daniel, N., & Boston, B. (1985). *Educating able learners: Promising programs and practices*. Austin, TX: University of Texas.

Farkas, G. (1996). *Human capital or cultural capital*. New York: Aldine De Gruyter.

Frary, R. (1995). *Testing memo 8: Reliability of test scores*. Blacksburg, VA: Virginia Tech Measurement and Research Services, Virginia Polytechnic Institute and State University.

Friedman, R., & Rogers, K. (1998). *Talent in context*. Washington, DC: American Psychological Association.

Graham, S. (1990). Communicating low ability in the classroom: Bad things good teachers sometimes do. In S. Graham & V. Folkes (Eds.), *Attribution theory: Applications to achievement, mental health, and inter-personal conflict* (pp. 17–36). Hillsdale, NJ: Lawrence Erlbaum.

Grimm, L., & Yarnold P. (1995). *Reading and understanding multivariate statistics*. Washington, DC: American Psychological Association.

Heider, F. (1958). *The psychology of interpersonal relations*. New York: John Wiley.

Herrnstein, R., & Murray, C. (1994). *The bell curve*. New York: The Free Press.

Hollingworth, L. (1942). *Children above 180 IQ (Stanford Binet): Origin and development*. Yonkers-on-Hudson, NY: World Book Company.

Howley, C., Howley, A., & Pendarvis, E. (1995). *Out of our minds: Talent development and anti-intellectualism in U.S. schools*. New York: Teachers College Press.

Iversen, G. (1991). *Contextual analysis*. Newbury Park, CA: Sage.

Johnson, R., & Wichern, D. (1998). *Applied multivariate statistical analysis*. Upper Saddle River, NJ: Prentice Hall.

Kelly, D. (1993). *Last chance high: How girls and boys drop in and out of continuation schools*. New Haven, CT: Yale.

Kinchloe, J., Steinberg, S., & Gresson, A. (Eds.). (1996). *Measured lies*. New York: St. Martin's.

Lareau, A. (1989). *Home advantage*. New York: Falmer.

Licht, B., & Dweck, C. (1984). Determinants of academic advantage: The interaction of children's achievement orientations with skill area. *Developmental Psychology, 20*, 628–636.

Marsh, H. (1984). *The self-serving effect (bias?) in academic attributions: Its relation to academic achievement and self-concept*. (ERIC Reproduction Service No. ED 252527)

Nunnally, J. (1967). *Psychometric theory*. New York: McGraw-Hill.

Nunnally, J., & Bernstein, I. (1994). *Psychometric theory*. New York: McGraw-Hill.

Oakes, J. (1986). *Keeping track*. New Haven, CT: Yale.

Paita, L., Love, D., Leftwachra, K., & Grabovsky, I. (1999, January). *Evaluating the analytic needs of HEDIS*. Paper presented at the National Association of Health Data Organizations, Atlanta, GA.

Pedhazur, E., & Schmelkin, L. (1991). *Measurement, design, and analysis: An integrated approach*. Hillsdale, NJ: Lawrence Erlbaum.

Peterson, C., & Barrett, L. (1987). Explanatory style and academic performance among university freshmen. *Journal of Personality and Social Psychology, 53*, 603–607.

Pressey, S. (1955). Concerning the nature and nurture of genius. *Scientific Monthly, 81*, 52–61.

Rotter, J. (1954). *Social learning and clinical psychology*. Englewood Cliffs, NJ: Prentice-Hall.

Rotter, J. (1972). Beliefs, social attitudes, and behavior: A social learning analysis. In J. Rotter, J. Chance, & E. Phares (Eds.), *Applications of a social learning theory of personality* (pp. 335–350). New York: Holt, Rinehart, and Winston.

SAS Institute. (1990). *SAS user's guide: Statistics*. Cary, NC: Author.

Sosniak, L. (1985). Learning to be a concert pianist. In B. Bloom (Ed.), *Developing talent in young people* (pp. 19–67). New York: Ballantine.

Stevens, J. (1996). *Applied multivariate statistics for the social sciences*. Mahwah, NJ: Lawrence Erlbaum.

Swartz, D. (1997). *Culture and power. Chicago*: University of Chicago Press.

Tabachnik, B., & Fidell, L. (1996). *Using multivariate statistics*. New York: HarperCollins.

Tacq, J. (1997). *Multivariate analysis techniques in social science research*. Thousand Oaks, CA: Sage.

Terman, L. (1925). *Mental and physical traits of a thousand gifted children*. Stanford, CA: Stanford University Press.

Tyler-Wood, T., & Carri, L. (1993). Verbal measures of cognitive ability: The gifted low SES student's albatross. *The Roeper Review, 16,* 102–105.

Velez, W. (1989). Why Hispanic students fail. In J. Ballantine (Ed.), *Schools and society* (pp. 380–388). Mountainview, CA: Mayfield.

3

The Crystallizing Experience: A Study in Musical Precocity

Cathy Freeman

Teachers College, Columbia University

This study examines the nature of musical precocity and the mechanisms that mediate a "crystallizing experience." Howard Gardner (1983) has made a cogent argument for the inclusion of musical intelligence in the spectrum of human intelligences. He has proposed that this musical ability may evolve in different ways. One of these is the "crystallizing experience," a dramatic event in a person's life that makes manifest inherent giftedness. The crystallizing experience may serve as a useful construct for explaining how certain talented individuals first commit themselves to an area of giftedness. The present study involved 24 musically precocious boys of middle school age who were asked questions, individually and in focus groups, regarding the nature of crystallizing experiences. This study of the crystallizing experience revealed important implications for understanding the structure and composition of extraordinary performance.

Editor's Note: From Freeman, C. (1999). The crystallizing experience: A study in musical precocity. *Gifted Child Quarterly*, 43(2), 75-85. © 1999 National Association for Gifted Children. Reprinted with permission.

W hat do we mean when we say that someone is "musically intelligent"? What propels a child toward high achievement in music? These questions have intrigued and baffled psychologists and educators for years.

In the last decade and a half, research on outstanding achievement and exceptional performance has proliferated (e.g., Ericsson & Charness, 1994; Howe, 1990; Simonton, 1988), and numerous books have been published on the topic of giftedness and multiple conceptions of talent (e.g. Csikszentmihalyi, Rathunde, & Whalen, 1993; Gardner, 1983; Gruber & Wallace, 1989; Feldman, 1980/1994). Of these, the work with the greatest relevance to the questions posed above is Gardner's *Frames of Mind: Theory of Multiple Intelligence* (1983), which introduces the term *musical intelligence.*

Gardner makes a cogent argument for the inclusion of musical intelligence in a constellation of seven distinct human intelligences of equal significance in human affairs. With this provocative combination of the terms *music* and *intelligence*, Gardner provides a new vocabulary and a promising conceptual framework for discussing and thinking about the nature and origins of musical talent and precocity. Precocious musical talent can now be seen as a manifestation of a high level of a separate and distinct human intelligence.

Gardner views emerging abilities as domain-specific, and he argues that exceptional talent results from a close match between an individual's intelligence profile and the demands of a particular domain. Gardner believes that exceptional talent can evolve in different ways. One pivotal factor in this evolution is the phenomenon known as the crystallizing experience (e.g., Walters & Gardner, 1986).

Putting the Research to Use

This manuscript contributes to the research literature on "crystallizing experiences," as defined by Walters and Gardner (1986). These findings support the notion of the crystallizing experience as a common phenomenon among the musically precocious. Of special interest are the reported long-term effects of the crystallizing experience on self-concept. The crystallizing experience can serve as a useful construct in identifying a potential area of giftedness or talent within a particular domain. Moreover, this construct could be useful in gaining insight into what students find intrinsically motivating, thereby optimizing the attainment of personal goals. This study also supports a trend toward multiple criteria for giftedness, in particular, Multiple Intelligence Theory approaches. Gifted and talented education is multi-dimensional, and the single conception of giftedness is indefensible. Asking children about the crystallizing experience opens up a new mode of inquiry and offers a new way of looking at what we do and how to meet the individual needs of gifted students.

THE CRYSTALLIZING EXPERIENCE

Following David Henry Feldman's earlier work on crystallizers of cognitive structures (Feldman, 1971, 1980/1994), Walters and Gardner (1986) defined the crystallizing experience as "a remarkable and memorable contact between a person with unusual talent or potential and the materials in the field in which the talent will be manifested" (p. 308). In other words, the person has a sudden moment of insight that sets the person on his or her life's course, a sudden illumination that dramatically affects the person's view of his or her ability within a given domain. For example, Debussy began his formal study at the age of 9, and by 14 he had won a prize for piano. During the first years, he did not show any interest in composition; however, all that changed when he listened to the music of Wagner (Walters & Gardner, 1986). Gardner wrote, "In speaking about crystallizing experiences, I have in mind moments when individuals have discovered their calling—something that is sufficiently sustaining so that they make a long term commitment to it" (personal communication, August 26, 1997).

Walters and Gardner studied biographical information about eminent individuals in mathematics, music, and the visual arts and interviewed teachers of talented students to identify trends and patterns that occur in the lives of creative people. Through their study of the lives of Galileo, Renoir, Debussy, and other great thinkers and artists, they uncovered a number of common characteristics and experiences. In many cases, the individual discovered an important aspect of his ability, or underwent a crystallizing experience, that seemed to yield a long-term change in his view of his ability within a given domain.

Although it seems that these experiences can take on various forms, they generally occur early in life and signal an affinity between an individual and some large-scale domain of interest. Walters and Gardner (1986) termed this the "initial crystallizing experience." Other experiences, or "refining crystallizing experiences," occur after an individual has undergone an initial attraction to the domain. In any case, Walters and Gardner reported that the dramatic nature of the crystallizing experience focuses the individual's attention on a specific kind of experience, and the individual is subsequently motivated to revisit these occasions in the future in order to reshape his or her self-concept on the basis of this experience.

Walters and Gardner's findings provide support for the construct of the crystallizing experience as a frequent phenomenon among the talented. However, it is possible to achieve a high level of talent in a domain like music through other means, such as an integration of biological heritage and intense training, as in the case of Mozart (Walters & Gardner, 1986). In short, Walters and Gardner did not prescribe the crystallizing experience as an inevitable antecedent or precursor of high achievement within a domain. However, it can serve as a useful construct for explaining how certain individuals may first discover their areas of giftedness and proceed to achieve at an exceptional level within a field.

The Crystallizing Experience and Gifted Education

Research on talent development and expert performance is highly relevant to the field of gifted education, especially as reflected in expanded conceptions of giftedness, such as the 1993 report from the National Office of Education. Research indicates that adult creativity is often foreshadowed by precocity in childhood and is sometimes concentrated in certain areas (Ochse, 1990), although most child prodigies never attain exceptional levels of performance as adults (Ericsson & Charness, 1994). These recent advances in understanding exceptional performance have, to date, had little impact on educational practice; they do not, for example, tell us how an individual may first discover potential talent.

The field of gifted education has yet to study in-depth a community of learners who are musically precocious and may have had crystallizing experiences. Such a study would do much to help us understand the conditions that precipitate and accompany the occurrence of experiences that, as Walters and Gardner (1986) argued, often play such a vital role in the development of domain-specific giftedness for some individuals.

Purpose of the Study

The purpose of this research is to determine whether crystallizing experiences were a common occurrence among a group of musically precocious boys, and, if so, what the nature, antecedents, and consequences of those crystallizing experiences were. Of particular interest and relevance to the present investigation is a strong, yet empirically untested conviction that the crystallizing experience has a dramatic lifelong impact on self-concept. The individual is subsequently motivated to revisit these occasions and make a long-term commitment based on these experiences. Specifically, I attempt to answer the following research questions:

1. Is the crystallizing experience a common phenomenon among the musically precocious; is it typical or atypical?

2. What kind of effect does this have on a young individual's life; is it one that is sufficiently sustaining to bring about an improvement in self-concept or an increase in ability within a given domain?

3. What is the nature of these experiences or their *raison d'être*? In other words, what are their internal structure, motivational aspects, and affective aspects?

4. What specific circumstances surround this particular event, and how does the initial crystallizing experience, which signals an affinity with a particular domain, differ from the refined crystallizing experience, which occurs later in life and marks the discovery of a particular instrument or style within a field?

METHOD

The present research employed data gathered from both qualitative interviews of individuals and focus groups to develop explanations and conclusions concerning the crystallizing experience as it relates to musical precocity. The research design used multiple methods of inquiry that contributed to the methodological rigor (Patton, 1990) of the study. This is in contrast to most studies that have assessed musical ability and its developments through standardized and criterion-referenced tests, measured through simple paper and pencil activities. Miles and Huberman (1994) contend that good qualitative data are more likely to lead to serendipitous findings and to new integrations. In the present research, I sought to allow dominant themes to emerge regarding the crystallizing experience, and in it I present retrospective accounts from the perspective of the student.

Research Site

St. Thomas Choir School is an independent school in New York City that was founded in 1919. The choir is governed by the rector and vestry of the St. Thomas Church and administered by the headmaster, who formerly served as headmaster of the Westminster Abbey Choir School in London, England. The Choir School was founded at the request of Dr. T. Noble, formerly an organist and chorus master at York Minster. Modeled on an English choir school, the St. Thomas Choir School marries the English choir school tradition to an American independent school and is the only church-affiliated boarding choir school in the U.S. and one of three remaining in the world. St. Thomas is not just a music school, but a fully accredited academic institution with an outstanding academic curriculum. In addition to preparing more than 400 pieces of music each year for six weekly choral services at St. Thomas Church on Fifth Avenue, the choir presents four or more annual concerts of major choral works with full orchestra. Religious and musical activities are important parts of the daily program. The choir, which has appeared on television at Lincoln Center and at Carnegie Hall, rehearses for 90 minutes each day.

Identification and admission are based on musical aptitude, scholastic ability, and probable adaptability to the life of the school, echoing somewhat Renzulli's (1986) definition of giftedness as above-average ability, creativity, and task commitment. Once a child applies for admission, the chorus master arranges a private audition, and qualified candidates are invited to spend a trial week at the school. The first step in the admissions process is the vocal and instrumental audition with the choir director, which serves as one of the measures for assessment of musical precocity. Academic and intelligence tests are administered after a trial week. Ten students who demonstrate high academic ability, unusual musical aptitude, and social-emotional ability strong enough to meet the rigorous demands that may befall children in a choir school setting are selected from a pool of students from the fifth grade.

Sample

The participants in this study were 24 middle school boys from the Choir School, ranging in age from 10 to 14, with a mean age of 12. The majority were Caucasian and of middle- to upper-middle-class backgrounds. As described in the previous paragraph, musical precocity is defined by a superior ability in both vocal and instrumental domains; this includes previous musical training in at least one instrument and the possession of a trainable soprano voice.

As an admission requirement to the school, the students were given the Wechsler Intelligence Scale for Children-Third Edition. The mean full-scale IQ for 24 children in the sample was 128. Other methods of academic assessment, such as previous achievement scores, were equally weighted in the students' overall academic profiles. The school screened and selected these students on their ability to meet the strong academic demands of the school.

Sample Selection

For the individual interviews and the focus groups, the participants were selected on the basis of a purposive sampling process, or what LeCompte and Preissle (1993) called criterion based selection. The sample was purposive "based on the assumption that one wants to discover, understand, gain insight; therefore one needs to select a sample from which one can learn the most" (Merriman, 1998, p. 48). The students were selected on the basis of their work, their musical aptitude, and what they could contribute to the questions being studied. For the individual interviews, the headmaster, music teacher, English teacher, and the author nominated seven students. For the focus groups, students from grades 6 and 8 were nominated based on the same set of criteria. A consent letter was sent to the parents of the students selected for the study. After receiving a signed consent letter from the student's parents, informants were chosen for the individual interviews. Confidentiality was secured by using a numbering system so that the student's anonymity was maintained.

Data Collection

The data for this study were collected over a three-month period and were derived from the following sources, 1) three 1-hour general observations at the research site; 2) single interviews with seven students; 3) two focus groups with intact English classes; and 4) conversations with parents to verify findings. Any documents and archival data that could illuminate the events that surround this particular event were reviewed. These consisted of admission files; admission test scores; report cards; teacher and parent comments; standardized scores; alternative measures of musical ability; correspondence; faculty memoranda; official correspondence between the school and parents; official school documents, such as school philosophy; the school publication, *Cantate*; newspaper articles; and examples of students' work.

The following methods served as a foundation for collecting the data and triangulating methods for the study: three general observations as a nonparticipant observer in the classroom (one hour each) augmented by a review of the site documents, school records, and evaluations; qualitative interviews (45-minute open interviews) with seven selected students; two focus group sessions (one hour each); and parent conversations to verify the students' statements. The multiple sources of evidence allowed for the "developing of converging lines of inquiry" (Yin, 1994, p. 92), one of the benefits of the process of triangulation.

General Observations

The first source of data included three hours of classroom observations and interviews with the classroom teachers. By working in the school on a full-time basis, I had unlimited access to the research site and school documents. I observed the students on three separate occasions and wrote field notes, which I later transcribed in a narrative text and studied for emergent themes.

Interviews. For the second source of data, seven boys were purposefully selected for the individual interviews by teacher nominations. The teachers selected the students based on their musical aptitude and their academic ability. The individual interviews provided an opportunity for deeper analysis and a chance to gain access to the subjectivity of the crystallizing experience. The students were interviewed individually in a quiet room in their school, and a friendly, conversational tone was maintained during the interviews.

The questions were scripted, and the students were asked the most important questions first, what Spradley (1979) referred to as the "grand tour" question. Following Patton's (1990) suggestion, I used open-ended, nondichotomous questions. Interview questions were structured before the single interviews and focus groups to guide the interview process. Breaking down questions and asking children about each component separately resolved difficulty in interpretation. To maintain consistency, the same language and terms were used in both the individual interviews and focus groups to describe the crystallizing experience. All single interviews were transcribed; none were tape-recorded. It was felt that the tape recorder might have diminished the quality of the conversational tone.

The students were given a typed copy of the following definition of the crystallizing experience: "A crystallizing experience is an experience that involves remarkable and memorable contact between a person with unusual talent or potential and the material in the field in which the talent will manifest" (Walters & Gardner, 1986, p. 308). When the students required further explanation, I explained that it was a memory that was sufficiently sustaining, one where they felt compelled to make a commitment to their musical ability.

Questions consisted of inquiries such as:

a. Have you ever had a crystallizing experience and how is it similar or different to the one described?
b. What kind of feeling did you encounter?
c. Who was present?

      d.   Is there musical ability in your family?

      e.   Did the crystallizing experience have a profound effect on your life? Did it change you in any way?

Focus groups. Following the individual interviews, two focus groups were conducted with two groups of 10 students in each (the mean age was 12). Three of the six boys from the single interviews were in the focus groups. The focus groups included students from both the eighth-grade and the sixth-grade English classes. Both the single interviews and the focus groups met for approximately 45 minutes and were guided by a similar set of questions.

LeCompte and Preissle (1993) recommended this method for discovering variation in people's responses and for revealing significant controversies among naturally bonded groups. Group interactions in this case tend to elicit more candid and explicit interpretations regarding the crystallizing experience.

LeCompte and Preissle (1993) suggested that the researcher should create a permissive environment in the focus group, which serves to nurture different perceptions and points of view without pressuring the participants to reach a consensus. Thus, at the beginning of each session, an effort was made to encourage comments of all types, both positive and negative. I was careful not to make judgments about the responses that might indicate approval or disapproval. The English teacher co-moderated the session by documenting key words and phrases. These notes were transcribed in narrative form and compared with my notes to ensure consistency of findings. The focus groups were tape-recorded, transcribed verbatim, and used for analytic induction (Miles & Huberman, 1994). Emergent themes were coded to ascertain the commonality in the crystallizing experience.

Data Analysis

In qualitative research, data analysis occurs throughout the study rather than during a period following the data collection. Data collection and analysis occur simultaneously (LeCompte & Preissle, 1993).

Miles and Huberman (1994) advocated a process-oriented approach called "Analytical Abstraction." Step one involves coding the data or packaging of the data, writing the analytical notes and linkages, followed by reconstructing interview tapes and written notes. Step two involves aggregating the data, identifying the themes and the trends in the data. Step three tests the propositions to construct an explanatory, framework. In other words, one begins with a text, codes the categories, identifies themes and trends, and then tests one's findings by creating an explanatory framework.

The present study employed the three-step process cited above: coding the data, aggregating themes, and recoding. This process was used in both the interview and focus group situations. In the first step, three copies of the data were made for both the single interviews and focus groups. The first set of copies were filed without notations to maintain an original in case it was needed later. Notes were written on the second set of copies of the individual interviews and transcribed notes from the focus groups. Such notes included questions that needed further probing and common themes that emerged. In the second step of the data analysis process, the data were coded to identify overall themes and trends. Notations were made in the margins to find emphases and gaps in the data. The third step of the data analysis process involved cross checking the data with the third set of copies for tentative findings. This procedure was used during data analysis to see patterns emerge through the use of triangulation.

The triangulation of the data requires the researcher to test one source of data to confirm or refute the value of the data's explanatory power. This technique helped to construct concepts, ideas and themes surrounding the crystallizing experience. Different typologies of the crystallizing experience and the relationship of the crystallizing experience to musical precocity were documented.

To facilitate presentation of the findings, field note recording forms captured the dialogue and were catalogued according to the questions. Synthesis was done by integrating the data into one explanatory framework. Under each question that guided the interview and focus groups, a section was provided for a brief summary, key points, and notable quotes to delineate major concepts and themes.

RESULTS

This exploratory study examined the nature of the crystallizing experience and the mechanisms that mediate its occurrence. Several themes emerged regarding the experience, both individually from the interviews and collectively from the focus groups. The results of the analyses of the crystallizing experience confirm previous findings that the crystallizing experience is a common phenomenon among the musically precocious. Of special interest are the reported long-term effects on the student's self-concept.

Research Questions

- *Is the crystallizing experience a common phenomenon among the musically precocious?*

The findings support the notion of the crystallizing experience as a common phenomenon among the musically precocious. Without exception, all seven boys in the individual interviews reported a crystallizing experience. Most of the boys in the focus group had a crystallizing experience. One student described his crystallizing experience as follows, "The most crystallizing experience for me was when I nailed the fourth movement of *The Pathetique Sonata*." Another student, describing his crystallizing experience, stated, "Well, music's biggest impact hit when I was six years old. I'll never forget it—the director told my parents that I had strong ability in the area of music." When asked how it felt, the student responded, "I don't think I could survive without listening or being around music. It felt like it was crystallized, glued to my body forever."

- *What kind of effect does this have on a young individual's life; is it one that is sufficiently sustaining to bring about an improvement in self-concept or an increase in ability within a given domain?*

Gardner wrote, "In speaking about crystallizing experiences I have in mind moments when an individual feels they have discovered their calling—something that is sufficiently sustaining so that they make a long term commitment to it" (personal communication, August 26, 1997). The most overt enthusiasm was given to the effect of this particularly powerful memory. When asked how it felt, the boys said, "Sometimes words can't describe it." One boy said, "It was like the light opened up. I'll never forget it." Another boy said, with tears in his eyes, "the experience was with my mom, it was just love . . . there is no other way to describe it." Arguably, it's a memory that has a dramatic effect; many boys felt the experience was profound, if not spiritual.

Of special interest are the reported long-term effects of the crystallizing experience on self-concept. When asked, most of the boys were eager to describe the experience. All of the boys in the groups, with the exception of one boy, reported having a crystallizing experience and stated that it improved their self-concept. Comments included, "From that moment, I knew I could do anything" and "I felt protected, secure, I'll never forget it." Statements such as, "I felt confident," "It increased my confidence," and "I felt I could do anything" were typical of the comments found in the interviews. As one student described it, "It's like when you fall on the ice with hockey equipment. You go down hard, but you feel protected; it's a weird feeling." Using another metaphor to describe the crystallizing experience, one boy said it was like "the Big Bang Theory."

- *What are its motivational or affective aspects?*

The construct of the crystallizing experience could be useful in gaining more insight into what students find intrinsically motivating. More important, this study suggests that the crystallizing experience may reveal potential areas of giftedness in certain domains that would have gone unnoticed in more traditional settings. The boys' accounts revealed an area of potential giftedness and an intrinsic desire to excel within a given domain. Six of the seven boys in the individual interviews had a crystallizing experience in the area of music, and one boy had it in the area of athletics. Interestingly, the boy who had a crystallizing experience in the area of sports demonstrated unusual ability in athletics. Walters and Gardner (1986) contended that it is consistent with the theory that many, if not most, will experience the affective phase of the crystallizing experience, especially if an individual is "at promise" within a particular domain. It is unlikely, according to Walters and Gardner (1986), that the experience will have a dramatic or lasting effect if the individual does not have some facility within the domain.

- *What specific circumstances surround this particular event and how does the initial differ from the refined crystallizing experience?*

Walters and Gardner (1986) hypothesized that the crystallizing experience can take on different forms. One is the initial crystallizing experience, which occurs early in a child's career and signals a general affinity between the individual and some domain of ability. One example is a three-year-old student who, after hearing "Happy Birthday" for the first time, played the initial chords an octave higher. The second is the refining crystallizing experience, which occurs later in life and helps the individual discover his or her own particular *métier* within a given domain of ability. The refining crystallizing experience is illustrated by the young adolescent who, while playing the piano, mastered the fourth movement of the *Pathetique Sonata*. The findings of this study suggest that, while the refining experience occurs later in training and typically under self-instruction, the initial crystallizing experience requires many resources, especially parental influence and early exposure to a musical instrument.

Consistent with previous findings, the initial crystallizing experience can serve as a way for an individual to enter a domain and, with the right conditions, achieve mastery of the domain, while the refining experience occurs after the individual has been attracted to the domain.

Parental support, practice, and exposure. Mastery of this ability is largely achieved through many hours of practice, exposure to the instrument, and parental support. Without these elements, the initial or refined crystallizing experience may not occur. Most of the boys agreed that their achievement had much to do with a combination of innate ability, practice, and hard work. Exposure to music and parental encouragement were germane to the initial crystallizing experience, while intensive practice was associated with the refining crystallizing experience. Several students indicated that the initial crystallizing experience would probably not have occurred without the support and encouragement of their mother, father, or teacher. They described parents who were supportive and encouraging of their talents. Comments such as "I remember my mom smiling at me" or "My dad was right there, I remember" were common in the interviews.

Most of the boys in this study came from musical backgrounds and were exposed to early training. Encouragement from a parental figure was a common theme when explaining the crystallizing experience in both the interviews and focus groups. However, praise or reinforcement was accepted only when the boys viewed it as honest and constructive. One boy who claimed that he did not have a crystallizing experience had memories of a demanding father. He stated, "I just wanted to get the piece over with." It seems possible that harsh memories can stifle the occurrence of the crystallizing experience. Walters and Gardner (1986) wrote:

The crystallizing experience is a fragile phenomenon that occurs principally when circumstances combine inborn talent, self teaching, and proper exposure to a set of materials in a particular way. Finally, in those circumstances where there is a strong predisposition to excel with a given material and where there is some but not exceptional opportunities, a crystallizing experience is most likely to occur. (p. 330)

Consistent with Gardner's findings, this study suggests that the crystallizing experience was a nearly ubiquitous phenomenon among these musically precocious boys. It should be highlighted as an extension of Gardner's previous findings that the boys were exposed to not only some, but to exceptional opportunities, which presaged the crystallizing experience. The role of maximal parental support and early instruction seems to be more important than innate talent (see Ericsson & Charness, 1994; Feldman, 1991; Howe, 1990).

Evidence from systematic research on prodigies provides little evidence for innate talent as the sole explanatory factor and demonstrates that exceptional abilities are often acquired under optimal environmental conditions. Feldman (1991, 1980/1994) argued that most child prodigies do not fulfill their potential in adult life because extreme talent, environmental support, the proper instructor, and chance rarely coincide. Talent is necessary but not sufficient for exceptional achievement in music; it cannot develop without extensive support, appropriate resources, and so forth (Feldman, 1991).

The musical instrument. An affinity with a particular instrument was a common theme in this present study and in previous research. Comments included, "I remember when I was playing a piano or violin??" One boy's crystallizing experience occurred when playing a piece by Beethoven at the piano. Another boy viewed his voice as an instrument. It seems the instrument represents the object of their inner expression. One boy said, "It just comes from inside. I can't help myself from singing." During a one-to-one interview, a student reported that his revelation occurred during a piano recital while his mother and piano instructor were present. The second experience occurred once while he played the clarinet. He said, "I'll never forget it. I was with my mother. We played *Etude Rose* in C major. My mom was there, I was, my teacher; the three of us were on stage."

Walters and Gardner (1986) discussed the importance of choosing an instrument, which can be considered fine tuning of a domain or finding a niche within a field. Several of these experiences described by the students sound like crystallizations themselves. In some instances, the boys described a moment in which they first came into contact with an instrument or the first time they came to the school and heard the choir. It was a moment that was so dramatic and sustaining that they made choices based on its single occurrence. Hearing the instrument sometimes crystallizes the sense of musicianship at a time prior to formal training.

The earlier recollections: The 10-Year Rule. The boys who had earlier recollections seemed to have distinctively unusual talent and demonstrated advanced musical aptitude based on teacher nominations and student comments. For example, one student stated, "When I was three years old, for my birthday, my mother played 'Happy Birthday.' I played the first couple of notes a few octaves higher." This student started to play his improvisations on the piano and began composing at the age of eight. He is currently writing an opera. Although he plays both the piano and cello, he feels more comfortable with the piano. Another boy, who is number one in choir, reported that his mother said she played classical music the day his parents brought him home from the hospital. One boy who plays the music of Mozart with superior skill was told that his mother played it continually before he was born. All reports were confirmed by the students' parents.

A further analysis revealed that each of the five boys who had recollections as early as three years of age have had almost 10 years of practice in music. Ericsson and Charness (1994) found that about 10 years of intense practice was necessary to achieve expert performance. Gardner (1983) contended that, irrespective of domain, it takes about 10 years of intensive practice to master a high degree of performance. Feldman (1980/1994) contends that a period of at least 10 years of work must occur before one achieves high levels of performance. Feldman (1991, 1980/1994) wrote, "For the music prodigy, the years from three to five are almost always crucial" (p. 54).

LIMITATIONS OF THE STUDY

There were some limitations to the present investigation. There is a potential bias in the sample selected. The students are musically precocious, middle school-age boys who come from unusually supportive backgrounds, which makes generalization difficult to students who are musically precocious with less supportive backgrounds. Future research should include a heterogeneous sample and other intellectual domains of ability. Additionally, the students are not only musically precocious boys, but are enrolled in a church-affiliated choir school. This presents an unusual challenge in terms of their fluency and ability to communicate such a private affair as the crystallizing experience. Unlike most middle school-aged boys, the boys studied here expressed their interpretations openly and treated the crystallizing experience as an epiphany or some dream-like revelation. The willingness of the participants to report the crystallizing experience may have been an indirect consequence of the context created in this highly unusual setting.

This study is also limited by the reliance on self-reports. It may have been possible that their descriptions were what they wished rather than what really happened. However, this seems unlikely, since parents, teachers, and friends confirmed the reports.

IMPLICATIONS

Implications for Theory

Walters and Gardner's interest in crystallizing experiences grew out of the Theory of Multiple Intelligence. The Theory of Multiple Intelligence (MI), as stated before, does not prescribe the existence or the importance of the crystallizing experience. However, it does suggest that these experiences occur across a variety of domains yielding sudden, powerful, long-term effects (Walters & Gardner, 1986).

More recent publications have challenged the legitimacy of these reports as memories that have become dramatized in the retelling due to their retrospective nature. Educators and psychologists have long been interested in the "Aha" experience. Howard Gruber (1981) presented a conceptually rich treatment of the "Aha" experience, which illuminated its complex inner structure. He viewed insight as a part of a protracted process, and he believed this process is regulated by purposeful work. In Gruber's study on "Aha" experiences, he measured insight through frequency, magnitude, and duration. He found, first, the occurrence of insight indicates a certain degree of mastery of the domain; insights often represent a moment of consolidation or confirmation. When the insight occurs, it is effectively laden in a way that accentuates the experience. Gruber questioned the validity of telescoping the essence of the creative process into a single moment or act such as the crystallizing experience.

Walters and Gardner (1986) described and listed exciting crystallizing experiences that set creative individuals on their life courses. These experiences came through contact with master teachers, parents, or, in some cases, exposure to an instrument (Ochse, 1990). According to Feldman (personal communication, June 10, 1998), the "Aha" experiences come in relation to solving a specific problem or resolving a specific conundrum. The essence of the crystallizing experience is similar, but not identical, to the "Aha" experience. Additional research is needed to determine whether Gardner's account of the crystallizing experience or Gruber's account of the "Aha" experience is the truer one, or whether each exists as a means of gaining insight.

The findings of this research provide evidence of the importance of examining the theorized instantaneous nature of the crystallizing experience. Although the students described this singular moment as one that was dramatic, a strong case can be made against the immediacy of such occurrences. Most students reported that their talent was largely due to vigilance, sacrifice, and hard work, and they felt that, without proper exposure, the initial crystallizing experience would not have occurred.

This brings us to the perennial question of talent versus training and how it applies to the crystallizing experience. Researchers in the development of expertise (e.g., Ericsson & Charnes, 1994) question the occurrence of the crystallizing experience and argue that differences in performance are altered by the amount of training received. In studying the lives of expert performers, they identify the central role of extensive focused training or deliberate practice. Gardner (1983; Walters & Gardner, 1986) argued that exceptional performance results from a close match between the individual's intelligence profile and the demands of a particular domain. According to the MI Theory, gifted children are children with a high degree of "raw" intelligence in a specific field who, under certain circumstances, demonstrate evidence of that intelligence before they are engaged in any kind of training regime (Walters & Gardner, 1986).

Recent evidence for the effects of training (e.g., Ericsson & Charness, 1994) has prompted some to question whether innate talents and specific gifts are necessary conditions for attaining the highest level of performance within a domain. Ericsson and Charness found that extended training alters the cognitive and physiological processes of experts to a greater degree than is commonly believed. Walters and Gardner (1986) and Feldman (1991) posited that the development of raw intelligence into the focus domain of expertise is as much a function of training as of raw intelligence. Similarly, Bereiter and Scardamalia (1993) acknowledged that talent influences the capacity to become expert, but they emphasized, along with Ericsson and Charness (1994), the time and effort needed to become an expert.

While it may not be necessary to demonstrate a genetic proclivity for attaining a high level of performance, the crystallizing experience can serve as a useful construct in identifying a potential area of giftedness or talent. Researchers in expert performance may question the utility of the initial crystallizing experience; however, a strong case can be made for the centrality of the refining crystallizing experience that occurs later in life after considerable training. The students in this study, however, also make a compelling case for the initial crystallizing experience as a genuine phenomenon that occurs early in one's musical career and signals a general affinity with some intellectual domain. Most students will experience the affective phase if they are at promise within a given domain.

Thus, on one hand it can be stated that early exposure to music is a prerequisite to the initial crystallizing experience. Through the initial crystallizing experience the individual's interest and motivation in and a domain become manifest in a commitment to instruction. The refining crystallizing experience, on the other hand, acts as a catalyst for further musical instruction, which may ultimately lead to the development of a very high level of expertise. For example, Yehudi Menuhin's crystallizing experience occurred when he was three years old. He was taken to concerts of the San Francisco Symphony regularly. "Upon hearing the sound of the orchestra and the violin played by Louis Persinger, he said, 'I asked for a violin for my fourth birthday, and Louis Persinger to teach me to play it.' He got both" (Walters & Gardner, 1986, p. 314).

The crystallizing experience, according to Walters and Gardner (1986), assesses the utility of multiple intelligences and brings that theory into contact with such issues as the inception of giftedness and how one achieves mastery within a domain.

Implications for Future Research

This study is the first step in providing information about the extent and nature of the crystallizing experience with musically precocious boys. Future research in other realms of intelligence and artistic domains and with heterogeneous samples would help extend the research reported here. Although Walters and Gardner (1986) contended that its occurrence varies across domains, further in-depth qualitative research is needed to ascertain the conditions that lead to a crystallizing experience. An important research strategy in identifying the crystallizing experience would emphasize the case study method. This type of retrospective account would allow for dialogue and a description of the process and conditions that give rise to creative insights.

Future research could focus on four primary objectives: 1) demonstrating a fit between the body of data for this study and understanding the crystallizing experience as it relates to a broader population or heterogeneous sample; 2) generating hypotheses about crystallizing experiences that are useful in identifying students potentially gifted in music and other domains of ability; 3) differentiating between what are termed initial and refining crystallizing experiences; and 4) examining further the inner structure of the crystallizing experience; is it revealed in a sudden illumination or is it part of a protracted process?

Implications for Practice

Educators would benefit if they viewed the student as able to achieve a crystallizing experience, which could thereby optimize the attainment of personal goals. Roeper (1996) wrote:

> Educators and experts in gifted education today see the gifted child in terms of what they [sic] do or are able to do and not who they are—not how their emotions differ from those of other children. They do not look at what motivates the child. (p. 18)

The concept of a crystallizing experience itself has a sense of "magic" that students are compelled to talk about. This construct could serve in gaining more insight and knowledge into the students' interests, hopes, and desires.

Roeper (1996) contended that "the gifted child has a complex self that is driven by his or her agenda" (p. 18). The crystallizing experience cogently captures what a student finds intrinsically motivating. Gifted children tend to develop an early internal locus of control, which tends to awaken this moment of clarity. It would be good pedagogy to question children about their crystallizing experiences, not for the good of society, but for the attainment of a personal goal.

Our field needs to recognize that the practice of gifted and talented education is multidimensional and that a single conception of giftedness is indefensible. Asking children about the crystallizing experience opens up a mode of inquiry and offers a new way of looking at what we do and how programs could be organized to meet the individual needs of gifted students.

REFERENCES

Bereiter, C., & Scardamalia, M. (1993). *Surpassing ourselves: An inquiry into the nature and implications of expertise*. Chicago, IL: Open Court.

Csikszentmihalyi, M., Rathunde, K., & Whalen, S. (1993). *Talented teenagers: The roots of success and failure*. New York: Cambridge University Press.

Ericsson, K. A., & Charness, N. (1994). Expert performance: Its structure and acquisition. *American Psychologist, 49*, 725–747.

Feldman, D. H. (1971). Map understanding as a possible crystallizer of cognitive structures. *American Educational Research Journal, 8*, 485–501.

Feldman, D. H. (1980/1994). *Beyond universals in cognitive development*. Norwood, NJ: Ablex Publishing Corporation.

Feldman, D. H. (1991). *Nature's gambit: Child prodigies and the development of human potential*. New York: Teachers College Press.

Gardner, H. (1983). *Frames of mind: The theory of multiple intelligences*. New York: Basic Books.

Gruber, H. E. (1981). On the relation between "Aha experiences" and the construction of ideas. *Historical Science, 19*, 306–324.

Gruber, H. E., & Wallace, D. B. (1989). *Creative people at work*. New York: Oxford University Press.

Howe, M. J. (1990). *The origins of exceptional abilities*. Cambridge, MA: Basil Blackwell.

LeCompte, M. D., & Preissle, J. (1993). *Ethnography and qualitative design in educational research*. New York: Academic Press.

Merriman, S. (1998). *Case study research in education: A qualitative approach*. San Francisco: Jossey-Bass.

Miles, M. B., & Huberman, A. M. (1994). *Qualitative data analysis*. Thousand Oaks, CA: Sage Publications.

Ochse, R. (1990). *Before the gates of excellence*. New York: Cambridge University Press.

Patton, M. Q. (1990). *Qualitative evaluation and research methods*. Newbury Park, CA: Sage.

Renzulli, J. S. (1986). *Systems and models for developing programs for the gifted and talented*. Mansfield Centre, CT: Creative Learning Press.

Roeper, A. (1996). A personal statement of philosophy of George and Annemarie Roeper. *Roeper Review, 19*, 18–19.

Simonton, D. K. (1988). *Scientific genius: A psychology of science*. New York: Cambridge University Press.

Spradley, J. (1979). *The ethnographic interview*. New York: Holt, Rinehart & Winston.

Walters, J., & Gardner, H. (1986). The crystallizing experience: Discovering an intellectual gift. In R. J. Sternberg & J. E. Davidson (Eds.), *Conceptions of giftedness* (pp. 306–330). New York: Cambridge University Press.

Yin, R. K. (1994). *Case study research: Design and methods* (2nd ed.) Thousand Oaks, CA: Sage.

4

Talent Beyond Words: Identification of Potential Talent in Dance and Music in Elementary Students

Susan Baum

College of New Rochelle

Steven V. Owen

University of Connecticut

Barry A. Oreck

ArtsConnection

We present evidence for the reliability and validity of the Talent Identification Instrument (TII), an observation process in music and dance in which multiple judges rate students throughout a multisession audition. The

Editor's Note: From Baum, S., Owen, S. V., & Oreck, B. A. (1996). Talent beyond words: Identification of potential talent in dance and music in elementary students. *Gifted Child Quarterly*, *40*(2), 93-101. © 1996 National Association for Gifted Children. Reprinted with permission.

approach was designed to recognize previously overlooked abilities in urban elementary students, including low income, bilingual, and special education students. The TII observation process was designed to evoke artful behaviors that can be readily recognized by arts specialists and classroom teachers.

We found strong agreement among raters and adequate stability estimates. Evidence for validity was obtained through factor analysis and a variety of construct validity procedures. The performance-based assessment described here may have implications for discovering hidden potential in academic as well as artistic domains.

Psychometrically sound assessment of talent in the performing arts has persistently challenged researchers. Lack of agreement on definitions and ratings of talent, even among specialists in a single discipline, has stymied accurate assessment. However, practitioners continue to rely on talent tests and performance auditions to select persons for talent development. Both approaches have special limitations for children who are disadvantaged or who do poorly on paper and pencil tests. For example, measures of music talent (e.g., Gordon Measures of Music Audiation [Gordon, 1979]; the Seashore Tests of Musical Aptitude [Seashore, 1938]) tap perceptual abilities in static contexts and require written responses.

Although auditions of performance seem preferable, they too tend to impose limitations. First, they offer constrained opportunities for talent demonstration. Single observations lack reliability and thus have little predictive validity (Nunnally, 1978). Researchers studying expertise have argued that motivation, task commitment, and creativity over time are as important as ability (Gardner, 1983; Renzulli, 1978). Further, motivation, task commitment, and creativity may be inhibited or impaired during a single audition.

Second, typical instruments used to evaluate musical and dance performance (e.g., Detroit Public Schools Creative Process Scale [Byrnes & Park, 1982]; the South Carolina Guidelines for the Identification of Artistically Talented Students [Elam & Doughty, 1988]) are sensitive to specific previous training. That is, they measure achievement not aptitude. This presents a particular validity problem for assessing children who have had limited opportunity for formal training in the arts.

Putting the Research to Use

This study is of particular importance and relevance to education because of current interest in the development of diverse talents in youngsters. It describes a culturally fair, reliable, and valid process for discovering music and dance potential in youngsters at risk, including bilingual, special education, and low income students. The process also sensitizes classroom teachers to the positive learning traits of students who may have had little previous success in school. When teachers observe such students sustaining attention, following complex directions, putting forth effort, and problem solving in dance or music activities, the teachers often raise their own expectations of students' abilities and adapt their teaching strategies to include music and dance activities.

Most important, however, is that this study provides a rationale for expending time and money on talent development in students at risk. Student success in a challenging arts training program—especially for youngsters struggling with school—may generalize to academic behaviors. Students learn how to sustain attention, exert effort, practice, be prepared, and commit to a goal.

Talent Beyond Words

Under a 3-year Javits grant from the United States Department of Education, ArtsConnection, a New York City agency, has aimed to identify and develop dance or music talent in elementary students. The ArtsConnection program, known as Talent Beyond Words, has the specific goal of targeting students who might be overlooked in conventional talent screening efforts. Further, this screening process was developed with particular attention to reducing cultural or socioeconomic bias in talent identification. The Talent Beyond Words screening process was developed and field tested in two Brooklyn, New York schools to identify third-grade students who show potential gifts and talents for dance and music.

The overall question that guided the research was: What is the evidence for reliability and validity of this talent identification process? In answering the question, we describe an observational model to identify potential talent in dance and music in children who are economically and academically disadvantaged. We also explain the development of an observational checklist for screening potential dance and music talent, and provide reliability and validity estimates for this procedure.

Definition of Talent

The talent identification process was designed to assess broad, behavior-based criteria that can be understood by both novices and experts in the arts. These talent criteria are listed and defined in Figure 1. Talent definitions that led to the observational instruments were developed by a panel of arts educators representing diverse artistic styles and techniques and included professional artists in music and dance. Panel members were selected by ArtsConnection in New York City, a prominent agency in arts and education.

METHOD

Subjects

Over 2 years, 15 third-grade classrooms ($N = 396$) from two New York City elementary schools with a substantial percentage of disadvantaged, bilingual, and special education students comprised the total sample. The ethnic composition of the two schools' third-grade classrooms was approximately 40% black, 37% Hispanic, 21% white, and 2% Asian. There were 52% males and 48% females. Four percent of the third-grade students in the sample were categorized as needing special education services.

The total sample was partitioned into three groups: selected, wait list, and not selected. The selected students were those who showed special talent, either in dance or music, during the audition process. Music talent was identified in students from one school ($n = 42$), and dance talent in students from the other ($n = 51$). Students in the wait list group showed potential but were inconsistent or borderline. There were 22 wait list dance students and 16 wait list music students. The final group, not selected, had 154 students who had tried out for dance, and 128 for music.

Identification Process

The procedure involved a multisession audition process that incorporated a broad array of activities to allow observation of many aspects of artistic talent. For 2 years, intact classrooms of third-grade students participated in seven consecutive weekly audition classes taught by a team of two professional artists (i.e., two dancers taught the dance classes, and two musicians, the music classes). The purpose of the audition classes was to select students with high talent potential for more advanced training.

During the audition classes, a panel of raters used an observational checklist called the Talent Identification Instrument (TII) to tally relevant student behaviors. The raters were the two professional artist instructors, the classroom teacher, an arts educator from ArtsConnection, and a different outside expert each week. The ArtsConnection rater has training and experience in the arts and in identification and development of talent in school-age youngsters. The outside experts were specialists in either the arts discipline or in gifted, bilingual, or special education.

Identification Process Curriculum

The curriculum for the audition classes combined technical and creative approaches. Lessons were designed to give students an introduction to the art form in an environment as similar as possible to an actual training class. Instructional methods were derived from various cultural traditions. They were designed to appeal to students from different ethnic backgrounds, to students who learn in different ways and at different speeds, and to students initially anxious or shy about the activities.

The dance curriculum for audition classes combined elements of modern dance technique, creative movement, and African and Caribbean dances and songs. Dance lessons involved warm-up routines, movement sequences and dance phrases, and solo and group improvisation. The music curriculum included rhythm exercises from many cultures, including Afro-Cuban, Caribbean, Asian, American folk, jazz and blues idioms, group and individual singing, and chants. The music classes blended methods from Orff technique with jazz improvisation, African percussion, and traditional music of the Gullah culture of the Georgia Sea Islands. Students worked on a variety of instruments, including xylophone, conga, bongos, hand drums, cymbal, and tympani. Each audition class had a different curricular focus designed to elicit a range of student behaviors indicative of potential in each of the talent areas. Recognizing the lack of prior arts instruction of many of the students, the audition served as an introduction to the art form as well as an assessment opportunity. The activities during the audition series became increasingly difficult, allowing for repetition of prior exercises and presenting challenges that required more than one session to master. This progression allowed for the observation of characteristics such as perseverance and recall and helped to counteract the effects of prior experience or initial shyness. Figure 2 shows the curricular focus of each session for dance and music.

Talent Identification Criteria

The TII consists of a class observation sheet and individual student talent profiles; both contain the talent behaviors to be observed. Outstanding performance in any area is marked with a simple plus mark next to the relevant behavior. The marks of the raters are totaled each week and a score is assigned based on the number of raters who noted the behavior during the class. The total score for an individual child is entered on the talent profile. An example of a talent profile for a selected student in dance for 7 weeks is shown in Figure 3.

At the end of each session the raters gave an overall rating that served as a tentative selection of students (selected, not selected, or wait list). The overall rating was an important feature of the TII system: It allowed the raters to consider

Figure 1   Key Words and Definitions for Identification of Talent in Dance and Music

DANCE

SKILLS

1. **Physical Control**
   knows by feeling; can make adjustments, can balance on one leg; has strength in legs, arms, torso; can maintain corrections
2. **Coordination and Agility**
   can combine movements, executes complex locomotor patterns, can isolate body parts from one another, moves freely through space, moves quickly
3. **Spatial Awareness**
   is aware of other people, adjusts to other dancers and the space, evens up the circle or line, is accurate in time and space
4. **Memory and Recall**
   remembers information, can perform without following, can see and replicate movements accurately, can build sequences
5. **Rhythm**
   puts the beat in the body, repeats rhythmic patterns accurately, anticipates, waits for proper moment to begin, can find the underlying pulse or beat

MOTIVATION

6. **Ability to Focus**
   directs attention, makes full commitment to the movement, is interested and involved in class
7. **Perseverance**
   doesn't give up easily, practices, improves over time, takes time to think, tries hard to get it right

CREATIVITY

8. **Expressiveness**
   shows pleasure in movement, performs with energy and intensity, is fully involved, communicates feelings
9. **Movement qualities**
   displays a range of dynamics; has facility moving in levels, directions, styles; communicates subtlety; moves fully; connects body parts
10. **Improvisation**
    responds spontaneously, uses focus to create reality, shows the details, gives surprising or unusual answers

MUSIC

SKILLS

1. **Rhythm**
   puts the beat in the body, is able to sustain an even beat, replicates rhythmic patterns accurately, can play repeating patterns, anticipates, waits for proper moment to begin, can find the underlying pulse or beat
2. **Perception of Sound**
   perceives differences in tone and pitch, responds to dynamics, can match pitches, can replicate melodic phrases, is able to sustain independent part
3 **Coordination**
   moves easily through space, able to do two or more things at the same time, can control body in movement and freeze, sustains repeating patterns, works with both hands

MOTIVATION

4. **Enthusiasm**
   responds joyfully, eager to participate, curious, asks questions, is open to unfamiliar styles of music
5. **Ability to Focus**
   directs attention, makes full commitment to the task, is interested and involved in class activities, listens carefully, follows instructions
6. **Perseverance**
   doesn't give up easily, improves over time, takes time to think, is able to take and use corrections

CREATIVITY

7. **Expressiveness**
   responds with sensitivity, performs with energy and intensity, is fully involved, communicates feelings
8. **Composition and Improvisation**
   improvises spontaneously, takes risks, makes surprising or unusual statements, creates sounds in original ways, makes up songs

additional impressions and to collect them into an overall appraisal. Strict numerical totals of observations on the tally sheet could not take into account the variety of talent profiles. Students who were outstanding in only a few areas would not receive as many tallies as those who were noticed in many areas but who may not have been outstanding in any one area. After the last audition session, the panel made their final selection for advanced training based on the total TII scores and overall impressions culled over the course of the auditions.

Another important feature of the process is the post-class consultation. A 10- to 15-minute discussion held immediately after the class allowed raters to compare observations and opinions, clarify vocabulary, and discuss other relevant student behaviors not specifically measured by the TII. The discussion also served the purpose of providing ongoing training in the use of the instrument for the teachers.

Instruments and Psychometric Evaluation

Two brief observational schedules—the Talent Identification Instruments (TII)—were developed, one for music (8 items) and one for dance (10 items) (see Figure 1). The TII evolved from the process ArtsConnection has used with over 15,000 students. TII's theoretical basis follows Renzulli's (1978) three-ring model of giftedness. In this model, giftedness results from interactions among three traits—above-average ability, creativity, and task commitment—and can occur in certain individuals, under certain circumstances, at certain times. In the arts, these three aspects of talent are highly related, merging intuitive, personal qualities with specific technical skills.

Because the TII was designed to be used in classes of 25 to 35 students, it was necessary to create highly readable and easily used forms with nontechnical language. For example, the term *motivation* was used as a functional substitute for *task commitment*. Final versions of the TII had 8 items for music (4 skills, 2 motivation, and 2 creativity) and 10 items for dance (5 skills, 2 motivation, and 3 creativity).

Reliability evidence for the TII included interrater estimates and 1-week stability estimates. Content and construct validity procedures included item review by expert artists in dance, music, and gifted education; factor analysis; convergent and discriminant evidence; and a contrasting groups comparison of talent ratings.

To examine the convergence between expert ratings (i.e., the TII scores) and teacher ratings, the *Teacher Searchlist for Spotting Talent (Searchlist)* (Baum, in press) was administered to the teachers. The *Searchlist* asks respondents to participate in a "search mission." They are given case descriptions of students who behave in ways that may signal gifted potential: learns easily, is curious and creative, is an avid reader, has deep interests, has spatial talents, shows leadership potential, is musically inclined, or demonstrates dance skills. If a description reminds teachers of a student in their classes, they note that child's name on the *Searchlist* and check the appropriate talent. The most checks any one

Figure 2   Curriculum Outline for Music and Dance Identification

Dance

Week 1 - Rhythm
   following and leading rhythmic patterns, improvising in time, across-the-floor patterns
Week 2 - Coordination and Agility
   mirroring, opposites, clapping and singing
Week 3 - Recall and Combine
   review of previous material and new combinations
Week 4 - Physical Control: Use of the Torso
   improvisations and spatial explorations involving energy in the torso
Week 5 - Spatial Awareness
   combinations, changing facing, creative explorations, across-the-floor; moving with others
Week 6 - Movement Qualities
   contrasting movement qualities, improvisation and composition
Week 7 - Focus (Silent Class)
   review of previous material, exploration of movement and isolation through imagery, observation and directed focus

Music

Week 1 - Rhythm
   replicating and repeating patterns, beat
Week 2 - Perception of Sound
   matching pitches, replicating melodic phrases, dynamic levels, sustaining vocal patterns
Week 3 - Songs and Melodies
   call and response, extended forms, singing, percussion in two or three parts
Week 4 - Phrasing
   knowing when to begin, transferring melodic phrases from voice to instruments, song forms
Week 5 - Coordination
   body percussion, control, using both hands, instrumental technique
Week 6 - Expressiveness
   percussion, improvisation and musical breaks, vocal inflection, movement
Week 7 - Composition and Improvisation
   improvisation within a given phrase, explorations of instruments, question/answer, sensitivity, intensity

student could receive would be eight. Baum (in press) summarizes psychometric evidence (reliabilities, content, and construct validity) for the *Searchlist*.

For discriminant validity evidence, we collected student scores on the Metropolitan Achievement Tests math NCE (normal curve equivalent) scores (MAT-Math) (Prescott, Balow, Hogan, & Farr; 1985/6); Degrees of Reading Power NCE scores (DRP) (New York State Department of Education and Touchstone Applied Science Associates, 1981); and the Piers-Harris Self-Concept measure (Piers, 1984).

Figure 3   Sample of Student Dance Talent Profile

Name ___Khadijah_____   CLASS ____O'Brien_____   SCHOOL ___Central_____

WEEK	1	2	3	4	5	6	7
PHYSICAL CONTROL	+ + + +	+ +		+ + + + +	+ +	+ + +	+ + + +
COORDINATION/AGILITY	+ +	+ +	A	+ + +	+ +	+	+ +
SPATIAL AWARENESS		+	B	+ +			+
RECALL AND OBSERVATION	+	+ +	S	+ + +	+ + +	+	+ + + +
RHYTHM	+ +	+	E	+	+	+ + +	+ + + +
ABILITY TO FOCUS	+ + +	+ +	N	+ + +	+ +	+ + +	+ + + + +
PERSEVERANCE		+	T	+	+ +	+ + +	+ + +
EXPRESSIVENESS	+ +			+ + +	+ +	+ + +	+ + +
MOVEMENT QUALITIES	+ +	+ + +		+	+ + +	+ + + +	+ +
IMPROVISATION		+		+ +		+ + +	+ + + +
SELECTION (1/2/3)	2.2	2.6		1.8	1.4	1.8	1.2
TOTAL SKILLS	8	8		14	8	8	15
TOTAL MOTIVATION	3	3		4	8	6	8
TOTAL CREATIVE	4	4		6	5	10	9

RESULTS

Content Validity Evidence

Content validity evidence for the instruments was obtained during the development phase. Originally designed by the ArtsConnection project directors, initial pools of 18 (for dance) and 16 (for music) observation items were generated based on Renzulli's (1978) conception of giftedness. The observational

Table I	Interrater Correlations of Audition Ratings		
	Music (n = 227)		
Rater	A	B	C
A	—		
B	.654	—	
C	.672	.788	—
	Dance (n = 192)		
Rater	A	B	C
A	—		
B	.782	—	
C	.813	.817	—

items and their definitions were then reviewed by six professional dancers and six professional musicians and were revised accordingly. The revised pools were then studied by eight persons with doctoral degrees in the field of gifted education, school district coordinators for arts and gifted education, and a psychometrician. The final TIIs contained 10 items for dance and 8 items for music.

Reliability Estimation

Mean interrater reliability estimates among three expert artists across 7 weeks ranged from .65 to .79 for music and from .78 to .82 for dance. Table 1 summarizes these interrater correlations.

Stability estimates for the TII were calculated over two separate 2-week intervals: between Weeks 1 and 2, and between Weeks 6 and 7. Stability estimates for music using the three expert raters ranged from .53 to .71. In dance, stability estimates ranged from .49 to .69. Because each week's sessions were designed to show different aspects of music or dance talent, we did not expect stability estimates to be high. These data show some consistency over time, like a general talent, but also some variation based on the specific demands of each session.

Criterion-Related Validity Evidence

Criterion-related validities were used to summarize convergent and discriminant evidence. We predicted that TII scores should be correlated with teacher *Searchlist* ratings of talent manifested in the regular classroom. Table 2 gives these correlations. For music, the average correlation was .40 ($r^2 = .16$, representing overlap in variance) between TII scores and teacher *Searchlist* ratings. In dance, the average correlation was .49 ($r^2 = .24$). These values are somewhat higher than the cross-construct values ($r^2 = .04$ and .13). The smaller cross-construct relationships were not unexpected, because both music and dance involve rhythmic and nonverbal expressive behavior.

Table 2   Validity Coefficients, Averaged over Both Years

	Dance TII (n = 227)		Music TII (n = 192)	
	r	r²	r	r²
MAT-Math-NCE	.25	.06	.08	.01
DRP-NCE	.11	.01	.08	.01
Searchlist-Music	.19	.04	.40	.16
Searchlist-Dance	.49	.24	.36	.13

For discriminant evidence, we predicted that TII talent ratings should be independent of academic achievement. Table 2 shows that these correlations ranged from .08 to .25 (r^2 from .01 to .06), showing little connectedness between these constructs. The small magnitudes of these correlations support the theoretical divergence of academic achievement and artistic talent.

Construct Validity Evidence: Factor Analysis.

To study the dimensionality of the TIIs, exploratory principal factor analyses were run for both the music and dance observational ratings (items summed across 7 weeks). In music, a single factor emerged, explaining 91% of the item covariation; the minimum loading was .75. The factor may thus be called Music Talent. Similarly, in dance, a single factor (Dance Talent) accounted for 89% of the covariation, with a minimum loading of .61. Table 3 shows the loadings of each item with its factor.

The factor results show that each set of observational ratings forms homogeneous, unidimensional composites. The strong loadings for all items also demonstrate simple structure in the data. Finally, the large amount of covariation explained for each analysis means that very little unsystematic variation exists in these observational data.

Construct Validation: Further Discriminant Evidence

Discriminant function analyses (DFA) were used to give a more comprehensive view of discriminant validity. To estimate the power of audition scores in the final selection of the students, DFAs were performed separately within dance and music to predict student status—selected ($n = 51$ and 42 for dance and music, respectively), wait list ($n = 22$ and 16), or not selected ($n = 154$ and 128). It was hypothesized that students' selections should be based on performance during the audition lessons rather than other factors such as classroom behavior, ethnicity, or academic scores. Various indicators of these (presumably)

Table 3   Factor Loadings for Dance and Music Items

Dance (n = 215)		Music (n = 183)	
Item	Loading	Item	Loading
2	.90	2	.91
4	.89	5	.90
1	.88	7	.89
9	.86	1	.88
6	.82	4	.82
8	.82	3	.82
5	.81	8	.79
3	.80	6	.75
10	.72		
7	.61		

irrelevant characteristics were gathered from student files. In traditional gifted and talented programs, classroom behavior and academic achievement are frequently used to identify giftedness. Indeed, when teachers are asked to nominate students for talent development programs, they often use such data. But under Javits Act Programs, grant recipients are expected to use nontraditional definitions for talented student selection. Thus we were interested in comparing the predictive worth of more traditional variables with the TII audition ratings.

The predictor variables were TII audition ratings from auditions, gender, ethnic group (dummy coded), Metropolitan Math-NCE, DRP-Reading NCE scores, and Piers-Harris Self-Concept subtest scores. In the DFA, only the TII ratings were significant ($p < .001$) in predicting group membership, and they explained between 61% (music) and 65% (dance) of the variation in group membership. According to Cohen (1988), these are very large effect sizes.

Construct Validation: Contrasting Groups Evidence

Additional construct validity evidence was gathered by collecting new TII ratings on selected and not selected students a year after the original audition process. A random sample of selected and not selected students from the Year 2 audition process participated in a new talent audition. The random selection aimed for a 30% nonproportional sampling (i.e., equal sample sizes) of selected and not selected students. The new audition was rated by professional artists unfamiliar with the Talent Beyond Words program. The dance students were judged on rhythm, coordination, movement, and overall talent; music students were rated on rhythm, coordination, focus, and overall talent. Within dance and music groups, a Hotelling T^2 was used to compare selected and not selected students on all TII ratings simultaneously. For dance students, there was a large overall difference between the TII scores of selected and not selected students ($T^2 = 29.01$, $p < .0001$). Univariate t-tests were used as a post hoc probe of the significant T^2 and are summarized in Table 4. To protect against inflated Type I error rate, a Bonferroni correction was applied to the alpha value: The nominal alpha of .05 was divided by 8 (t-tests), to give a new alpha of .006. The t-tests (Table 4) show that selected students dependably received higher TII ratings. For music students, there was also a large overall difference ($T^2 = 32.80$, $p < .0001$). As with dance students, the univariate t-tests favored selected students for each rated behavior.

Construct Validation: Informal Supplementary Data

One of the most significant markers of the success of an assessment approach is its ability to predict future performance. During the 2-year advanced training for selected students in the Talent Beyond Words program, we had opportunities to observe the development of individual student potential. According to semiannual evaluations by arts instructors using the identification criteria, 80% of the students made good to excellent progress. Although the training was rigorous, only 9% of the students left the program. Additional evidence of identified students' readiness for advanced training was seen in the high attendance rate during audition classes, the amount of home practice claimed, and instructors' reports of students' on-task behavior during their arts classes. Perhaps the most practical measure of accomplishment is that these students have been invited to perform at many school, community, and city-wide events, culminating with a performance at the 1993 Presidential Inaugural celebration in Washington, DC. Several students were selected to participate in the annual Walt Disney Music Camp, a national program for young talented musicians. Another was selected to compete in Japan in an international competition sponsored by the Nippon Corporation. These and other achievements are even more remarkable considering the students' lack of previous arts training and performing experience.

Discussion

Preliminary data from the identification process described here show promise for developing a psychometrically sound means of identifying dance and music talent in students at risk. This is particularly timely considering the current emphasis in education on identifying and nurturing multiple intelligences (Gardner, 1983). Selections also were based on audition performances rather than on factors such as classroom behavior, ethnicity, or academic scores. Thus, this talent identification process appears to be relatively free of cultural and economic bias.

Student success in a challenging arts training program—especially for youngsters struggling with school—may generalize to academic behaviors. First, we speculate that success experiences in the arts may raise student,

Table 4   Blind Ratings After One Year of Training

| | DANCE (selected n = 15; not selected n = 16) | | | | |
	_M_	_SD_	_t_	_df_	_p_
RHYTHM					
Selected	14.7	1.4			
			4.89	29	.0001
Not Selected	11.5	1.3			
COORDINATION					
Selected	14.8	1.4			
			4.94	29	.0001
Not Selected	11.2	1.5			
MOVEMENT					
Selected	15.1	1.5			
			4.89	29	.0001
Not selected	11.5	1.4			
OVERALL TALENT					
Selected	44.6	3.8			
			5.40	29	.0001
Not selected	34.0	3.9			

| | MUSIC (selected n = 13; not selected n = 14) | | | | |
	_M_	_SD_	_t_	_df_	_p_
RHYTHM					
Selected	22.4	3.4			
			5.53	25	.0001
Not Selected	14.5	4.4			
COORDINATION					
Selected	21.9	3.6			
			4.05	25	.0004
Not Selected	13.4	4.6			
FOCUS					
Selected	21.8	3.3			
			4.05	25	.0004
Not selected	17.1	2.6			
OVERALL TALENT					
Selected	66.1	9.8			
			5.32	25	.0001
Not selected	44.6	11.8			

teacher, and parent expectations: There was widespread surprise that students "incapable" of sustained attention and task commitment could persist in, and succeed at, a difficult program. Perhaps, flush with success, students will test their improved self-efficacy in new applications. Second, there should be specific self-regulatory behaviors that do transfer to new environments. For example, attending carefully to a dance demonstration is analogous to watching a teacher demonstrate a math solution on the chalkboard. We are now collecting student self-regulation data—in arts and in academic behaviors—to test this hypothesis.

It may be argued that the reverse could just as well be true: Success in academic areas might generalize to arts performance. We respond that these two domains do not have reciprocal influence. These students, in general, have had little history of academic success. Whatever their schools, teachers, and parents had tried had not had much influence in instilling competence or confidence. By contrast, new opportunities to show different sorts of skill seem to have given these students—at least the selected ones—the sorts of successful experiences and expectations that can reverse continued failure in an academic environment.

In summary, talent in dance or music comprises many related subskills: physical abilities, coordination and agility, motivation, expressiveness, and improvisational skill. The identification process developed, tested, and reported for this project elicited these behaviors to provide a dependable assessment of performing arts talent. The success of this approach in identifying talent in diverse populations suggests a new approach to discovering aptitude frequently overlooked by teachers and standardized tests. The multisession, multifactor approach described here shows promise and may have implications for discovering hidden potential in academic as well as artistic domains.

REFERENCES

Baum, S. M. (in press). Recognizing talent in young children. In S. M. Baum, S. M. Reis, & L. Maxfield (Eds.), *Developing talent in young children*. Mansfield Center; CT: Creative Learning Press.

Byrnes P., & Park, B. (1982). *Creative products scale: Detroit public schools*. Paper presented at the Annual International Convention of Council for Exceptional Children, Baltimore, MD.

Cohen, J. (1988). *Statistical power analysis for the behavioral sciences* (2nd ed.). Hillsdale, NJ: Lawrence Erlbaum.

Elam, A., & Doughty, R. (1988). *Guidelines for the identification of artistically gifted and talented students* (rev.). Columbia, SC: South Carolina State Department of Education.

Gardner, H. (1983). *Frames of mind*. New York: Basic Books.

Gordon, E. (1979). *Primary measures of music audiation and intermediate measures of music audiation*. Chicago: GIA.

New York State Department of Education and Touchstone Applied Science Associates. (1981). *Degrees of reading power*. New York: College Board.

Nunnally, J. C. (1978). *Psychometric theory* (2nd ed.). New York: McGraw-Hill.

Piers, E. V. (1984). *Piers-Harris children's self-concept scale, revised manual.* Los Angeles: Western Psychological Services.

Prescott, G. A., Balow, I. H., Hogan, T. P., & Farr, R. C. (1985/6). *Metropolitan achievement tests* (6th ed.). San Antonio, TX: Psychological Corporation.

Renzulli, J. (1978). What makes giftedness? Reexamining a definition. *Phi Delta Kappan, 60,* 180–184, 261.

Seashore, H. (1938). *Psychology of music.* New York: McGraw-Hill.

5

Talent Beyond Words: Unveiling Spatial, Expressive, Kinesthetic, and Musical Talent in Young Children

Sandra I. Kay

State University of New York at New Paltz

Rena F. Subotnik

Hunter College–City University of New York

Talent Beyond Words was developed to identify and serve children with potential talent in the performing arts, especially dance and percussion music. Participants in the program included elementary-aged students

Editor's Note: From Kay, S. I., & Subotnik, R. F. (1994). Talent beyond words: Unveiling spatial, expressive, kinesthetic, and musical talent in young children. *Gifted Child Quarterly*, *38*(2), 70-74. © 1994 National Association for Gifted Children. Reprinted with permission.

attending two inner city schools. All pupils at targeted grade levels received instruction over several weeks in order to provide rich opportunities for dynamic assessment by teams of professional artists, arts educators, and specially trained teachers from participating sites. Students identified as a result of the audition processes took part in demanding after-school curricula over the course of 3 years. The students' proficiency levels in their respective performing arts were impressive, as was the esteem they gained from teachers, classmates, parents, and from their own disciplined efforts.

INTRODUCTION

The fourth floor of PS 130 is unseasonably hot, and bright sunlight pours in from old fashioned auditorium windows. Fourteen sixth graders who form the Talent Beyond Words (TBW) jazz percussion group have been practicing for over an hour. There are no signs of restlessness or boredom. Complete concentration and nervous excitement will carry them through two more hours of a demanding rehearsal agenda.

Interspersed among the students are adult performers from the New School for Social Research. David Pleasant, professional musician and conductor of the TBW group, ensures that his instrumentalists provide rhythmic support for other group members and coaxes them to personalize the music with improvisation. Several youngsters with prodigious musical talent have emerged from this melange of ages, talents, and instruments. Equally as important, the entire student ensemble has been provided with rare opportunity to exercise disciplined study and practice in a valuable, cultural endeavor.

PROGRAM DESCRIPTION

Background of the Project

The nonprofit organization that sponsored and created the TBW project has been offering arts programs to adults and children for the past 14 years. The offices and studios, currently housed in the former High School of Performing Arts building immortalized by "Fame," offers classes, consultations, and professional development to individuals, corporations, and schools. The staff for this program consists of arts administrators, professional dancers, musicians, and other performing artists who have a special interest in sharing their talents and skills.

The staff and administration of ArtsConnection, led by Steve Tennen and Barry Oreck, developed and modified an identification process for artistic talent ripe for testing in the most challenging of educational environments. In cooperation with PS 130 and PS 27 in Brooklyn, New York's Community School

District 15, and with educational consultants Susan Baum, Edith DeChiara, and Jane Remer, Oreck developed TBW supported by a United States Department of Education Javits Grant. Dance and music were the performing arts selected for the project because those areas are usually absent from the skill repertoire of regular classroom teachers and because they matched well with the expertise available at ArtsConnection.

The TBW plan was designed "to help build a nationwide capability in elementary and secondary schools to identify students who are potentially artistically gifted and talented in dance and music, and to meet their underserved educational needs" (Oreck, 1993, p. 2), especially in underrepresented populations. A second goal was to provide third and fourth graders with services related to musical arts and dance arts. Third and fourth grades were selected as the intervention point for the Javits project for the following reasons: (a) the experience would prepare the students to compete successfully for places in special secondary arts programs; (b) rigorous music and dance performance training traditionally begins at these early ages; (c) the stigma associated with boys involvement with dance would not yet be overwhelming; and (d) music and dance skills would help develop coordination and poise in children entering adolescence. PS 130 and PS 27 offered a large population with special educational needs, including bilingual and low income students, that could test TBW identification procedures and program design.

The specific objectives designed to achieve the goals of TBW included:

- preparing all children in Grades 3 through 5 for participation in the talent identification and audition process by providing extended exposure to music or dance art forms;
- collecting and contributing empirical evidence to the growing body of knowledge about the identification, selection, and education of the artistically gifted by expanding upon the Gardner, Renzulli, and other models, including instruments and techniques developed by ArtsConnection;
- arriving at new, functional, and operational definitions of giftedness and talent in dance and music useful to educators as well as experts;
- providing artistically talented students with in-depth opportunities to work with professionals in the field.

The young performers that stood before us on the stage had been judged by a team that included their classroom teachers, professional artists, and arts educators at the beginning of the TBW project (3 years earlier) to have untrained talent for musical performance. The creative force emitted from the performers and spilling off the small stage energized the entire auditorium. The data collected for the present report helped explain the magic that engaged our senses.

The Experimental School Sites

The experimental schools are located in two Brooklyn, New York, neighborhoods. PS 130 has a diverse socioeconomic population of students including students requiring bilingual services. The students are mainly from the Spanish- and French-speaking Caribbean and from the former Soviet Union. During the first year of the grant project (1990), 201 students were included in the music audition process. The core talent group selected from these two grades included 45 students: 18 Black, 16 Latino/a, and 11 White. Among these 45 were 3 special education students. Slightly more boys than girls were identified for services.

PS 27 is located in a much lower income neighborhood than the other experimental site. The student body tends to come from local public housing projects, and is less socioeconomically and ethnically diverse. From the 195 students in the third and fourth grades in 1990, 51 were chosen as the core group for dance instruction. Twenty-nine of the core group members were Black, 21 Latino/a, and 1 White. Three were also from special education classes. The percentage of students identified for dance services favored girls.

The Identification Model

The identification model was derived from the work of Gardner, Renzulli, and ongoing research conducted by the TBW team. Gardner provided the conceptual framework for recognizing music, kinesthetics, and spatial reasoning as full-fledged areas of human intelligence worthy of encouragement in school children. Gardner's multiple intelligence theory (1983) supports the notion of individual talent that can be developed in young children in each of those areas.

Renzulli's three-ring conception of giftedness (1986) provided a rationale for the work derived empirically by the TBW research. Above-average intelligence from the Renzulli three-ring concept was modified to represent *physical and cognitive skills* in music and dance. *Motivation* was operationalized as persistence and was particularly noticeable if a child remained actively enthusiastic beyond the first three to four audition sessions, when the novelty of breaking school routine might be exhausted. *Creativity* was translated into individual expression and cooperative problem solving in music or dance. The specific criteria adapted from the three-ring model are summarized below:

Process of Identification

Through a series of workshops held during summers, weekends, after school, and at lunchtime, teachers were trained by professional artists and art educators to serve as judges of dance or music auditions. All children in the third and fourth grades at the two schools were provided with seven lessons based on essential skills in dance or music taught by professionals in varied ethnic contexts and artistic styles. The objectives of this extended audition process were to expose all students to the art forms initial skills and to provide a series of informed practice sessions from which student responses could be categorized according to mastery of the criteria listed in Figure 1. Each week, each student was rated on his or her response to the lesson, so that each student

Figure 1   Talent Identification Criteria for Dance and Music

Dance	Music
SKILLS	
physical control	rhythm
coordination and agility	perception of sound
spatial awareness	coordination
observation and recall	
rhythm	
MOTIVATION	
ability to focus	enthusiasm
perseverance	ability to focus
	perseverance
CREATIVITY	
expressiveness	expressiveness
movement qualities	composition and improvisation
improvisation	

From Baum, Owen, & Oreck (1993). Adapted by permission.

was given seven trials in seven contexts to demonstrate his or her potential. The classroom teachers and TBW personnel associated with each school site served as judges over the course of the seven sessions, and visiting experts ensured that ratings were unbiased by earlier student auditions.

How TBW Fits into the Existing Paradigm for Educating Artistically Talented Children

A coherent program of instruction in the arts is one that addresses "the issue of general learning essential for all students and special learning for particular students who choose them" (Reimer, 1992, p. 45). There is a way of

> thinking and knowing unavailable except by being (or acting as) an artist. All students need to share this cognition for the sake of knowing what it uniquely allows one to know. . . . The special learning segment of the arts curriculum is, on the other hand, essentially selective and intensive. (Reimer, 1992, pp. 46–47)

Two levels of art programs are needed in the schools: one for all children and one serving the artistically talented (Wakefield, 1992). Yet most elementary schools choose to spend whatever limited resources are available responding to the first level by offering minimal exposure to selected art forms to all students, leaving the development of the artistically talented to secondary schools or families utilizing outside resources. Although expertise in some disciplines (e.g., dance, music) must begin at an early age, public programs for artistically talented students at the elementary level are virtually nonexistent, leaving two critical gaps in artistic/aesthetic education in the public domain.

Finite time and resources, coupled with course offerings limited to the traditionally Western European fine arts, has prompted many community-based organizations to collaborate with schools in providing experiences in the "heritage arts" or other popular art forms (Mitchell, Wolf, & Philip, 1993). The formats of these programs, however, tend to be (a) one-time exposure of a cultural art form to an entire student body (assemblies), (b) integration of the arts into the regular classroom curriculum through a thematic approach (Beckwith, Garfield, Halley, Jones, & Porter, 1992), or (c) artists-in-residence type enrichment (including heritage artists) offered at the secondary level (Mitchell et al., 1993). Following the elimination of arts education positions in many schools (especially in city systems), a program such as TBW that provides all three approaches at the elementary level is unique. Differing slightly from other exemplary arts-in-education programs (such as the Lincoln Center Institute and its sister programs), TBW emphasizes long term, in-depth curriculum modification for artistically talented students once they are identified.

The identification of artistically talented students has been historically problematic (Carroll, 1987; Kay, 1982). Assessment has been based on products or performance that depict developed skills, a procedure appropriate for secondary students who have the requisite interest and training (or, at least, practice). A method for assessing raw potential talent has not previously been available. TBW offers a novel approach in that its identification framework introduces a baseline of skills in a particular art form to all students. From this point, a set of criteria (not based on developed skills) is employed by a panel of experts to identify potential artistic talent in music or dance. Researchers in gifted education have suggested this type of identification procedure (Renzulli, 1986; Tannenbaum, 1983), especially with regard to the artistically talented, yet schools consistently identify students whose creative products reveal obvious past experience with the talent area (Mitchell et al., 1993). The TBW project has provided a model worthy of review, reflection, critical analysis, and further exploration, especially by those currently involved with national assessment standards for arts education.

DATA COLLECTION AND SUMMARY

The qualitative data that provide the basis for this report were collected from two on-site visitations, a review of program documents, and the draft evaluation document submitted by the external evaluator of the grant. The on-site visits included opportunities for observation as well as interviews with teaching faculty, guidance counselors, parents, administrators, and students directly involved with the program at PS 130 and PS 27, and with Barry Oreck, the TBW co-director.

The interview questions were designed to elicit an overall context for viewing program components. Teachers and counselors learned from professional artists and art educators how to conduct an audition and were extremely enthusiastic about acquiring this new evaluation skill. They were particularly comfortable with a process that gave every child an opportunity to be identified. The parents of TBW identified students described the new poise and confidence demonstrated by their children and their renewed interest in school attendance. The administrators were delighted with the excellent public relations gained by their schools and the pride of the entire student body in the accomplishments of their talented classmates. Students voiced a feeling of mastery acquired from working as respected peers with adult performers. Finally, the director expressed his satisfaction in establishing and testing a long-dreamed-of educational project.

PROGRAMMATIC OUTCOMES

Four outcomes of the program were identified by TBW staff and validated both by grant-funded evaluators and by the present observers:

Established a model process to identify youngsters with potential talent for dance and music. The identification method designed for the TBW project has been adopted and used successfully by the staff of two public schools in collaboration with professional artists and arts educators. The staff expressed confidence that students selected using this process benefited from the rigorous training component of the program based on increased school attendance, enthusiasm for the arts, and invitations to perform for a wide array of public audiences. The process is inclusive, in that every third- and fourth-grade child in each school was auditioned and given every opportunity to demonstrate musical or dance talent. The screening process extended over a 7-week period and included various judges, further ensuring equal opportunity of discovery.

An integral part of the assessment method was the participation of classroom teachers. Mean interreliability estimates among the professional artists for student audition ratings were .79 for music and .81 for dance. After 6 weeks of staff development, including observation, and extensive discussion and guidance on the part of professional musicians and dancers, interrater reliability of student audition ratings between teachers and professional experts was .63 in music and .71 in dance (Oreck, 1993).

Expanded classroom teachers' ability to see a wider range of talents among their students and to value the importance of full integration of the arts into elementary education. Teachers are traditionally focused on the cognitive talents of their students, particularly in terms of mastering the basic skills of reading and mathematics. In the two schools combined, 62% of the identified students were reading below the 50th percentile; 26% were reading below the 25th percentile.

At PS 27, 82% were below the 50th percentile, and 38% were below the 25th percentile. In mathematics, the combined mean scores for identified students in both schools was 34% below grade level, with 6% in the lowest quartile.

Teachers reported that before TBW they were inclined to see most of their students as having learning difficulties. However, witnessing the replication of complicated dance patterns after a single demonstration revealed to these teachers the children's previously hidden capacity for memory and sequencing. Grace and poise replaced teachers' impressions of lack of control and restlessness. According to the participating teachers, although there were no direct effects on academic outcomes, classroom ambiance changed with the new respect accorded to core group students by teachers and peers. For example, one fourth grade teacher stated: "This program gave them a purpose. They began to have that 'I belong-type gleaming.' If they can feel good about themselves, they can do anything." Another teacher at PS 27 who served as program director expressed delight in observing children change from "poorly disciplined fighters with low self-esteem, to ladies and gentlemen in the dance, context."

Reflecting their inadequate preparation for arts instruction, teachers stated that before the onset of TBW they infrequently used the principles and skills derived from those disciplines in the classroom. Because of their growth in confidence as well as training in the arts, these classroom teachers felt comfortable integrating the arts to some degree into the school day for all of their students. One special education teacher, for example, described how creative movement now helps her students move in an orderly fashion through the halls.

Integrate parents into the process of nurturing and identifying talent. As reported by school staff, parents were rarely involved in school activities prior to the arrival of the TBW project. By the end of the third year, parents were far more visible in the school—assisting at rehearsal, attending performances, participating in parent workshops, and offering support to one another.

Provide an opportunity to experience disciplined and rigorous effort toward accomplishing a valuable cultural goal. Most regular elementary school programs focus inordinate energy on basic skills. Because traditional gifted programs tend to serve students who readily master basic academic skills, those programs often provide exposure to topics beyond the regular curriculum. Opportunities for multiple-year immersion in a discipline are rarely offered (Subotnik, Kassan, Summers, & Wasser, 1993). The experience of mastering the first hurdles of physical awkwardness and new vocabulary require long hours of concentrated effort. Only a small minority of children are involved in such endeavors, either in sports or in classical music, and, typically, such endeavors are arranged by parents. The TBW project integrated hard work with musical and dance talent, resulting in a powerful experience for participating students within and beyond the confines of the school.

AREAS FOR FURTHER EXPLORATION

Interviews with parents, students, administrators, support personnel, and teachers at PS 27 and PS 130 revealed two general attitudes that remain essential to further work in gifted education. First and foremost, there was little sense of elitism associated with the TBW weekly pull-out program of advanced study or with the participants in the core group. This model provided exposure to basic artistic skills for all students, and selected from that experience students for intensive talent development. The reduced perception of elitism may have been enhanced by the program's focus on the arts rather than on academics. Furthermore, the general public tends to find it far more palatable to support specific talent rather than global intellectual giftedness. The question remains: Would the general perception of appropriate education for academically gifted students be supported if programs paralleled the TBW method by addressing specific abilities in mathematics, science, and humanities? In a climate in which the national trend is to eliminate academic programs, this question is worthy of exploration.

The second perception that prevailed throughout our interviews is one of intense commitment to the basic importance of art in the school curriculum. One homeless child had been identified for the core group. Although the daily life of her parent was preoccupied with basic survival, the mother saw to it that her child participated in the extended rehearsal hours and performances that were required in this program. The pride felt by the entire family during a performance warranted the extra effort.

Another intriguing discovery was reported by Barry Oreck in the course of discussion about the identification process. He noted that the TBW staff ascertained that children who came into the program with strengths in the creativity criteria could rather easily be taught to meet the skill criteria. On the other hand, those children who came in meeting the skill criteria had far more difficulty developing their creativity.

David Pleasant, professional musician and music instructor for the TBW project, indicated that all the students were challenged by expressing themselves in the arts. However, in the course of developing their expertise, students varied as to when and how much challenge they were interested in pursuing. Integral to his teaching style, Pleasant provided options so that choosing a more difficult task was left up to the motivation of the students. When a student requested a challenge, it was provided. These observations are supported in research on the nature of expertise in the arts (Kay, in press) and in research indicating that the organization of instruction for high-ability students must involve an elevated level of discovery-oriented structure in the learning environment (Snow, 1993).

The 3-hour rehearsal is over. It is May 13th, and the school year is coming to an end, particularly for sixth graders in a K-6 school. The next day, the percussion jazz ensemble from PS 130 will perform masterfully at Bryant Park.

A large and noisy lunchtime crowd of office workers and managers will collect around the bandshell to enjoy and marvel over the talents of the mixed aged musical group. The musicians still bask in the acclaim they have already received at the Inaugural celebration of President Clinton. All the ensemble members have been invited to study with professional musicians at the New School for Social Research on weekends during the next academic year. One boy has joined the Disney World orchestra, and three girls and three boys will be touring with David Pleasant as part of his professional group. The future seems ripe with possibilities.

REFERENCES

Baum, S. M., Owen, S. V., & Oreck, B. (1993, April). *Talent beyond words: Identification of potential talent in dance and music in elementary school*. Paper presented at the annual meeting of the American Educational Research Association. Atlanta, GA.

Beckwith, B., Garfield, W. T., Holley, C. M., Jones, J. C., Porter, S. E. (1992). Tribal rhythms: A thematic approach to integrating the arts into the curriculum. In M. R. Goldberg & A. Phillips (Eds.). *Arts as education* (Reprint series # 24) (pp. 67–78). Cambridge, MA: Harvard Educational Review.

Carroll, K. L. (1987). *Towards a fuller conception of giftedness: The arts in gifted education and the gifted in art education*. Unpublished doctoral dissertation. Teachers College. Columbia University, New York.

Gardner, H. (1983). *Frames of mind*. New York: Basic Books.

Kay, S, (1982, February). Gifted and the arts: A prismatic view. *School Arts*, pp. 16–18.

Kay, S. (in press). The nature of expertise. In R. Friedman & F. Horowitz (Eds.), *Proceedings of the 1992 Esther Katz Rosen Symposium*. Washington, DC: American Psychological Association.

Mitchell, R., Wolf, D. P., & Philip, F. (1993). *Issues concerning a national assessment of arts education*. Washington, DC: The Council of Chief State School Officers.

Oreck, B. (1993). [Program evaluation report]. Unpublished raw data.

Reimer, B. (1992). What knowledge is of most worth in the arts? In B. Reimer & R. Smith (Eds.), *The arts, education, and aesthetic knowing: Part II, ninety-first yearbook of the National Society for the Study of Education* (pp. 30–50). Chicago, IL: University of Chicago Press.

Renzulli, J. (1986). The three-ring conception of giftedness: A developmental model for creative productivity. In R. J. Sternberg & J. E. Davidson (Eds.), *Conceptions of giftedness* (pp. 53–92). New York: Cambridge University Press.

Snow, R. (1993, May). *Aptitude development and talent achievement*. Keynote presentation at the Henry B, and Jocelyn Wallace Research Symposium on Talent Development. Iowa City, IA.

Subotnik, R. F., Kassan, L. Summers, E., & Wasser, A. (1993). *Genius revisited: High IQ children grown up*. Norwood, NJ: Ablex.

Tannenbaum, A. J. (1983). *Gifted children*. New York: Macmillan.

Wakefield, J. F. (1992). *Creative thinking, problem-solving skills, and the arts orientation*. Norwood, NJ: Ablex.

6

Identifying Artistically Talented Students in Four Rural Communities in the United States

Gilbert Clark

Enid Zimmerman

Indiana University

Project ARTS was designed as a research and development project to identify high-ability, artistically talented third graders from four different ethnic backgrounds in seven rural schools and to implement differentiated arts programs for them. Locally designed identification measures, developed by teachers and community members, were found to be appropriate by teachers and staff if several different measures were used. In research about identification of students for Project ARTS, scores on the Torrance

Editor's Note: From Clark, G., & Zimmerman, E. (2001). Identifying artistically talented students in four rural communities in the United States. *Gifted Child Quarterly*, 45(2), 104-114. © 2001 National Association for Gifted Children. Reprinted with permission.

Tests of Creativity, Clark's Drawing Abilities Test, and state achievement tests were found to be correlated. Except at one site, gender was not found to be a significant variable on these tests. It was recommended that local measures, the CDAT, and achievement tests be used to identify artistically talented students in rural communities with populations similar to those in Project ARTS.

In recent years, there has been a focus on special programs for students in urban environments. The needs of students from rural communities throughout the United States are often less visible and certainly less well reported, although they also require educational programs designed to meet their special needs. Books and journals about educating gifted and talented students are filled with references to programs and advantages offered to urban and suburban students because most educational opportunities for students with high abilities have been offered in cities and the areas surrounding them (i.e., Freeman, 1991; Swassing, 1985; VanTassel-Baska, 1988, 1998). There are few visual or performing arts programs or projects for high ability visual arts students from distinctly rural communities, with ethnically diverse backgrounds, offered in year-round local schools (Bachtel, 1988; Leonhard, 1991).

Although much has been written about identifying students with high academic abilities, there has been a paucity of research about identifying artistically talented students, art talent development in general, or about programming for artistically talented students, particularly from rural backgrounds (Clark & Zimmerman, 1994). There have been some measures designed to identify high-ability students in the visual and performing arts, although identification measures of visual arts talent for under-represented groups need further research and development before they can be used to advantage. Definitions used in such programs should be broad and open-ended because it is important to be expansive when seeking or identifying high-ability performance levels in rural schools without previous programs for artistically talented students. Restrictive identification measures, such as specific creativity or achievement test scores, are often used in urban or suburban school districts. Certainly, such cut-off scores would *not* be appropriate to use in most rural schools, particularly those serving economically disadvantaged or ethnically diverse students; few students would be accepted into art talent development programs on the basis of these types of test scores.

Because of their distance from large population centers, students in rural schools often do not have easy access to traditional cultural resources such as large art galleries, major museums, comprehensive libraries, concert halls, and similar facilities found in major urban areas (Spicker, Southern, & Davis, 1987;

Nachtigal, 1992). Students from rural schools, therefore, do not have the same exposure to, or opportunities to explore, the kinds of arts resources and experiences available to students in more heavily populated urban and suburban parts of this country, although they often have rich cultural heritages and strong community support networks. Torrance (1997) claimed that most identification measures require that children respond in terms of experiences common in the dominant, advantaged culture.

Putting the Research to Use

Identification of artistically talented students is an area of gifted and talented education that needs more attention through research and development activities. Especially missing from identification programs in the United States are identification measures adapted for rural populations. In this article, a number of local and standardized measures are suggested for identifying students in rural areas with potential or who evidence high ability in the visual arts. Also of interest for those who wish to adapt identification programs for rural schools is the demonstrated correlation of academic and art talent abilities as evidenced on the Clark's Drawing Abilities Test and state achievement tests. For those who will be identifying artistically talented students in rural schools, it is suggested that a number of different local and standardized measures be used in any identification process, such as teacher-developed measures, a standardized achievement test, and a standardized art test.

Schools seeking to identify high-ability visual arts students in smaller, rural communities usually have not identified enough students to warrant specialized teachers, appropriate instructional resources, or access to mentors (Bolster, 1990). At this time, there is a great need for development of valid and reliable identification instruments and other measures to facilitate broad talent development in a variety of contexts for all students with high abilities in the visual and performing arts. This is especially true for students with art talent potential and abilities who live in smaller, rural communities across the United States.

In a monograph published by the National Research Center on the Gifted and Talented, we offered a number of recommendations for future inquiry about the identification of artistically talented students that are directly applicable to programs in rural communities (Clark & Zimmerman, 1992). These included: (a) the identification of high-ability visual arts students should be based on attention to student potential and work in progress, as well as final performances and products; (b) development of effective alternatives to standardized testing, such as process portfolios, work samples, and biographical inventories, because most standardized tests are not appropriate for identification of students with high abilities in the visual arts; (c) study of students' backgrounds, personalities, values, and age as factors in identification of art talent; and (d) use of diverse multiple-criteria systems in all identification programs for artistically talented students, with an emphasis on measures of various aspects of students' backgrounds, behaviors, skills, abilities, achievement, personalities, and values.

PROJECT ARTS

In an effort to serve the many needs of artistically talented students in rural schools, from economically disadvantaged and/or ethnically diverse backgrounds, Project ARTS was designed as a three-year research and development project to identify underserved, high-ability, visual and performing arts students in grade 3 in selected rural schools and to implement and assess differentiated visual and performing arts programs appropriate to these students during the succeeding two years. Project ARTS was funded from 1993 to 1996 by the Javits Gifted and Talented Students' Education Program. All schools participating in Project ARTS served 55% to 99% of their students free or subsidized lunches, indicating by federal standards that their local communities were economically challenged.

Major purposes projected for Project ARTS were to: (a) design, modify, and demonstrate identification instruments and procedures appropriate to rural students from Appalachian, European, Hispanic American, Native American, and African American backgrounds; (b) modify and demonstrate visual and performing arts curriculum models and materials differentiated for use with high-ability, elementary school students from these populations; and (c) modify and demonstrate evaluation instruments and procedures to assess the progress and achievements of students from the identified populations.

It was a Project ARTS policy to avoid directive interventions into the climate, organization, nature of identification procedures, or arts offerings at each cooperating school. Locally designed identification programs and curricula were developed at each site based on general policies and guidelines described for all Project ARTS schools. These guidelines were to: (a) be sensitive to local cultures and learner characteristics of specific groups of students at each site; (b) use locally developed measures, procedures, and criteria; (c) be inclusive of many visual and performing arts skills; and (d) be based on several, clearly different kinds of measures and procedures. In addition, the locally developed identification programs were to be designed by specific school personnel at each site. Due to space limitations, we will be discussing only the identification procedures developed for the Project ARTS visual arts programs.

METHODOLOGY

Project ARTS staff began testing more than 1,000 students in the third grade in seven specific rural schools, with input from advisory groups of teachers, parents, administrators, artists, and other concerned community members. These advisory groups were established before the testing to offer advice about local populations and appropriate expectations for students in each community. Students in the third grade at all participating schools were administered an entire range of local measures adopted at each site. In addition, at the end of the second year, evaluators at each school interviewed staff, teachers, students, parents, and community members about their perceptions of identification measures used at each site.

The Project ARTS staff also required each school to administer two standardized instruments, a modified Torrance Tests of Creativity and Clark's Drawing Abilities Test, that were used for research purposes only. Schools that initially were to participate in Project ARTS were chosen because of their previous connection with another Javits Grant for academically talented students. Unfortunately, due to political and other impediments, none of the schools that participated in the original academic project were able to cooperate. Fortunately, alternative sites were established in the original states, and some staff from the original Javits academic project did participate (Clark, 1993).

Site Descriptions

Cooperating schools included two schools in Indiana in two different communities. Both are in rural, agricultural, southern Indiana where people claim predominantly Scottish-Irish, German, and/or Native American ancestry. There also are direct relationships to southern Appalachian backgrounds in both school populations. For several generations, people in these two communities lived in relative isolation before modern industrialization and development encroached into the region. Both schools are in economically challenged, low-growth communities, with few resources for attracting new development.

Two schools in New Mexico, with students from different cultural backgrounds, participated in Project ARTS. Most students' backgrounds in one school reflected Spanish, Catholic traditions intermixed with and influenced by inter-marriages and commerce with Native Americans from nearby pueblos. The other cooperating school was on a pueblo with an entirely Native American population. This is a traditional, conservative pueblo that strives to protect and preserve its cultural traditions through a number of practices. All visitors to the pueblo, for instance, are required to leave the pueblo before 5:00 p.m., and most official communication in the pueblo is conducted in *Keres*, the local native language.

Located near the southern, coastal tip of South Carolina, the other three schools are located in a community on the sea islands, populated by people of Gullah descent. They serve a community population and rural schools populations. The sea islands have been home to African American people who created the Gullah culture since the earliest days of the importation of African slaves into South Carolina.

Local Identification Procedures

Currently, there are no agreed upon criteria derived from research findings about the validity of using, or interrelationships between, local identification measures, such as open-nominations, structured nominations, grades in art classes, academic records, locally designed tasks, portfolio reviews, interviews, or in-class observations (Brooks, 1997). These measures, nevertheless, frequently are recommended for use in school identification programs for gifted and talented students. Many states have prepared specific guidelines for identification of artistically talented students (Bachtel, 1988), and a number of these states, including Indiana and South Carolina, advocate use of such multiple-criteria systems, based on using many and diverse measures (Elam, Goodwin, & Doughty, 1988; Keirouz, 1990).

The issue of how to identify accurately artistically talented students in diverse, underserved populations in rural communities was a concern for the Project ARTS staff. Students from rural areas and diverse ethnic, economic, and social groups often possess unique characteristics that should be taken into consideration when identification procedures are being developed or selected (Baldwin, 1984; Zimmerman, 1992, 1994). All students differ in their interests, learning styles, learning tempo, values, motivation, habits, and personalities, as well as their ethnicity, gender, economic backgrounds, and social backgrounds. All of these characteristics generally are ignored in formal reports of scores on standardized arts-related or academic tests.

For the populations being served by Project ARTS, a problem arose as to whether high abilities should be defined only as being able to create superior visual arts products or perform in a distinguished manner. It was decided that attention also should be paid to potential talent development that might lead ultimately to advanced products from students who lacked resources or experiences similar to those offered in more urban or suburban schools and who, typically, might not receive high scores on standardized tests.

Early in the calendar of Project ARTS, leaders of groups from all three states attended an identification workshop. The goal of this workshop was to encourage each site to develop local identification measures that would be sensitive to each school's population in order to select high-ability, rural students into Project ARTS programs. Each site and cooperating school was encouraged to require as many identification tasks or measures, related specifically to their local populations, as they deemed necessary. At each Project ARTS school, local committee members' advice about what constituted art talent in each of their communities was taken into consideration when identification measures were formulated.

Locally Designed Measures

Although each site developed local identification instruments, many of the measures used did not vary across the schools or states and fell into predictable categories often recommended in gifted and talented literature. On the other hand, several tasks at each site were designed specifically as local identification measures for specific populations (See Table 1).

Table 1   Local Identification Procedures Used in Indiana (IN), New Mexico (NM), and South Carolina (SC)*

	IN	NM	SC
Self-nomination forms	•	•	•
Parent nomination forms	•	•	•
Teacher nomination forms	•	•	•
Peer nomination forms	•	•	•
Collage/design work sample task			•
Storyboard for teacher-read story			•
3-D clay animal task			•
Student attitude questionnaire			•
Sketchbook (for summer use)		•	
Other standardized class assignments	•		
Community art exhibition		•	
Student porfolios	•	•	
Out-of-school projects	•		
Observations of students (in classes and on field trips)	•		
Previous art grades	•		
Achievement test scores	•		•

Note. * These procedures do not include the Torrance Tests of Creativity or Clark's Drawing Abilities Test

Indiana Identification Procedures. Identification methods used in Indiana schools included 10 locally designed measures, including nominations by students, parents, teachers, and peers; student portfolios; out-of-school projects; previous art grades; observations of students; achievement test scores; and written research proposals. These measures were designed to be as inclusive as possible, and results were charted in one school to create individual student profiles. Grading criteria were developed locally at each school, and student scores were recorded for each measure.

One Indiana school used a museum field trip as a unique identification procedure. Volunteers, parents, and teachers recorded students' behaviors and responses at the museum on a form designed by the art teacher. At this school, all peer nomination forms required both boys and girls be listed in response to each of a number of descriptive statements about art talent. It was felt that stereotypic role definitions were learned early in this rural community, and many peer selections might result in single sex groupings.

New Mexico Identification Procedures. Methods used in New Mexico schools included seven locally designed measures: nominations by students, parents, teachers, and peers; summer sketchbooks; a community art exhibition; and student portfolios. Procedures of special interest in New Mexico were use of a summer sketchbook, a community art exhibition, and nominations by a local artist-teacher. Summer sketchbooks were distributed at the end of the school year to all third graders in both schools, who were asked to return them with drawings and other notations at the beginning of the next school year. Although only a small percentage of sketchbooks were returned, those that were indicated high interest and commitment by students who completed them.

All students in one New Mexico school were invited to submit art work for a community exhibition. This exhibition was held at a local gallery and judged by local adult artists on a set of commonly agreed upon criteria, including originality, technique, and composition. In the pueblo school, a local artist, who also was an official of the pueblo community and employed as an artist-teacher with Project ARTS, had worked with many of the students for several years, knew their art work well, and nominated a number of them to participate.

South Carolina Identification Procedures. Methods used in South Carolina schools included nominations by students, parents, teachers, and peers; a collage/design work sample task; storyboards for a teacher-read story; three-dimensional clay animal work samples; student attitude questionnaires; and achievement test scores. Three unique local measures and criteria, resulting in work samples, were developed to be sensitive to cultural influences of students from Gullah backgrounds. Because pattern and design are important to artists from this area, one was a torn-paper collage design. Storytelling is another art form deeply embedded in the Gullah culture, and a second procedure called for all students to illustrate a story in a sequence of four prepared panels. These also were judged, with locally developed criteria, by art teachers in the cooperating schools. A third procedure involved having all students make clay animal figures because this task might be sensitive to skills of rural students who often use found materials to experiment with ideas and create three-dimensional objects.

IDENTIFICATION INSTRUMENTS AND PROCEDURES USED FOR RESEARCH

There are few nationally standardized tests available to measure drawing abilities, and tests that do exist have been questioned as to their usefulness because of outmoded items, inadequate samples, weak validities, inconsistent scoring, or incompleteness (Buros, 1972; Eisner, 1972). Most state art achievement instruments do not require students to produce art work or answer questions about the arts; they often contain only verbal multiple-choice items without illustrations due to printing costs and the expense of scoring (Hamblen, 1988; Sabol, 1994). These situations raise questions about identifying high-ability art students in rural populations that may not emphasize standard language, arts skill development, or provide frequent standardized testing experiences.

Standardized Instruments

A number of standardized identification measures were considered for use in Project ARTS, including the Torrance Tests of Creativity (TTC), Clark's Drawing Abilities Test (CDAT), and state achievement tests. During this project, scores on these three measures were used only for research purposes due to cooperating school districts' rules about confidentiality. Scores obtained on TTC, CDAT, and state achievement tests were given anonymous codes so that they could not be compared with scores received on local identification measures.

Torrance Tests of Creativity. An abbreviated Torrance Tests of Creativity (TTC) was administered specifically to assess use of this test for identifying high-ability students in schools with rural, culturally diverse populations. TTC scores have often been used as identification measures for visual arts programs in urban and suburban settings in the United States (Bachtel, 1988; Torrance, 1997). Torrance's staff at the University of Georgia approved the abbreviated TTC used in Project ARTS as a reliable indicator of creativity. This abbreviated version consisted of three tasks: (a) list as many unusual uses of junked automobiles as you can; (b) make some pictures (in four, preprinted rectangles) and make up titles for your pictures; and (c) see how many objects you can make from 12 preprinted triangles on a page. This TTC was used as evidence of skills of fluency, flexibility, and elaboration. Subjects received a numeric, quantitative score on the TTC based upon completion of these tasks. All Torrance tests were graded by trained Project ARTS staff at Indiana University. Results obtained with the TTC are summarized in Figure 1.

Clark's Drawing Abilities Test. Many researchers believe art talent is relatively stable, is normally distributed, and that the amount of talent a person develops will effectively control and limit his or her capabilities in the visual arts. In other words, all students possess talent, but some will develop it to a small degree, most to an average level, and some will develop it to considerable heights (Clark, 1989). To test these beliefs, an instrument was required that would demonstrate common differentiations of art abilities among students based on the work sample technique. Work samples require completion of the same task, using the same amount of time, with the same materials and instructions by all students in order to compare student performance. Completion of the same task by all students provides a more legitimate basis for analyzing and comparing children's art development than an examination of different products rendered in a variety of media.

Development of the CDAT to measure various levels of children's drawing abilities was motivated by previous inquiry and speculation about the abilities and development of artistically talented students. Study of past assessments of children's drawing abilities and design and testing of possible items was conducted for several years toward development of an instrument that could be

Figure I   Distribution Obtained With Torrance Tests of Creativity

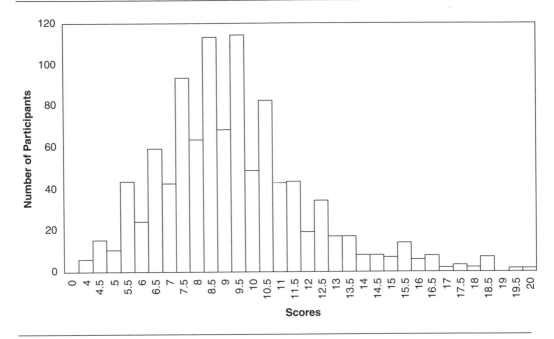

Note. SD = 2.67; M = 9.32; N = 1.021

used to categorize students' art work into differential ability groupings and test the assumption that art talent is normally distributed. The resulting CDAT has been shown to be reliable and valid and has been used widely in schools in the United States and in a number of other countries (Clark, 1992).

The CDAT consists of four items in which subjects are asked to: (a) draw an interesting house as if looking at it from across the street; (b) draw a person running very fast; (c) draw a group of students playing on a playground; and (d) make a fantasy drawing from your imagination. Directions also call for a 15-minute time limit on each task. Some previous versions of all of these items have been used in earlier studies of children's drawing abilities, and each requires differing sets of abilities and skills (Clark, 1992). Items a, b, and c specify subjects to be drawn; item d is open-ended and self-generated.

Past uses of the CDAT have been analyzed and reported based on age, gender, grade, and SES demographic data about subjects and in relation to achievement scores (Clark & Wilson, 1991). General school populations clearly yield differentiated ability levels, including levels for high-ability students. As more and more subjects have been tested, evidence has accumulated that drawing ability, as a measure of talent in the visual arts, is normally distributed in school populations. The CDAT was administered to all third-grade students in all schools cooperating with Project ARTS because it previously had been successfully used to identify differentiated ability levels among elementary students.

Standardized State Achievement Tests. In addition to TTC and CDAT, Project ARTS students also were administered standardized achievement tests as part of each district's testing program. These tests were idiosyncratic for each state, thus scores across sites cannot be compared. Results of these tests can be compared in each state, however, with results from the TTC and CDAT. Achievement tests used were: (a) in Indiana, the Indiana Statewide Testing for Educational Progress (ISTEP); (b) in New Mexico, the Iowa Test of Basic Skills (ITBS); and (c) in South Carolina, the Stanford Achievement Test (SAT-8). These tests were administrated to all students in each school and coded results were accessible from school records.

RESULTS AND DISCUSSION

During 1993–94, all of the cooperating schools identified, using local measures, specific groups of students with the potential for high ability in the visual and performing arts for participation in Project ARTS. The median group size was approximately 30 students at each school. Results on local measures used in each school or community were discussed with the Project ARTS staff, although actual data were not shared. Groupings of students who were identified for the project and who performed well on local measures were visited and observed on several occasions by Project ARTS staff during the subsequent two years. When Project ARTS students' progress and achievements were assessed after the project was concluded, there was evidence that most students chosen for the program developed skills and understandings about art and increased their awareness and appreciation of the arts in their local communities.

Locally Generated Identification Measures

It was expected that locally generated identification programs would be successful generally because of their sensitivity to local cultures and characteristics of students at each site, use of locally developed procedures and criteria, inclusiveness of appropriate visual arts skills, and use of a variety of information and measures. In addition, these locally developed identification measures were designed by teachers in their own rural schools, with input from parents, community members, artists, administrators, and consultants, based on their shared perceptions of local strengths and needs. It was anticipated that generalities about identification of visual arts students in rural schools from diverse backgrounds derived from this inquiry would help form a research base from which other communities would be able to develop programs for different populations of students with similar interests, potential, and abilities in the visual arts.

Schools cooperating with Project ARTS created a number of local identification programs that reflected recommendations for identification of artistically talented students in rural communities. In interviews by Project ARTS staff members, a few teachers expressed concern about using some of the tasks (even though these were locally designed and administrated) and expressed faith in their own perceptions of students' abilities, based on observations of past performance. In other words, even though these teachers were asked to develop and administer unique, local measures and completed this task, a few were unsure about how to assess the results, lacked faith in the validity of their own assessment abilities, and sometimes rejected using the results as selection devices. The majority of teachers, however, felt the local measures were appropriate for identification of artistically talented students in their rural schools. The most successful identification measures, according to staff observation and teacher endorsements, were work samples, community exhibits, teacher observations, and self-nominations. Today, many schools served by Project ARTS continue to use some of the instruments and experiences developed locally to identify students with high abilities in the visual arts.

Research Results of Standardized Tests

Analysis of variance (ANOVA) was used to assess the results on achievement test scores, although these are reported specifically only for each state because each state used different tests. TTC and CDAT scores were compared to the gender of subjects, and these also are reported by state. Acceptance levels of inter-judge correlations, standard deviations, and ranges of scores were determined by reference to Anastasi (1998) and Linn and Gronlund (1995).

TTC and CDAT Scores. An abbreviated Torrance Tests of Creativity (TTC) was administered to 1,021 students in grade 3 at all seven schools participating in Project ARTS. These TTC were scored by three trained judges at Indiana University, and an inter-judge correlation of .86 was calculated by use of the Pearson product-moment correlation. The mean score on the TTC was 9.32, with a standard deviation of 2.67. The range was 0–20. Scores on the TTC indicated a wide range of creative behaviors as defined by this measure. Although skewed somewhat to the left (as expected in schools with an economically challenged population and little exposure to arts resources), the scores were distributed relatively normally; some scores were at the low range, most were at the mid-range, and some were at the high range, as shown in Figure 1.

Clark's Drawing Abilities Test (CDAT) was administered to 946 students in grade 3 at all seven schools participating in Project ARTS. The CDAT was scored by three trained judges at Indiana University and an inter-judge, Pearson product-moment correlation of .85 was calculated. The mean score on the CDAT was 73.2, with a standard deviation of 29.96. The range of scores for each item was 0–200. Distribution of scores on the CDAT identified a broad range of differentiated

Figure 2   Distribution Obtained With Clark's Drawing Abilities Test

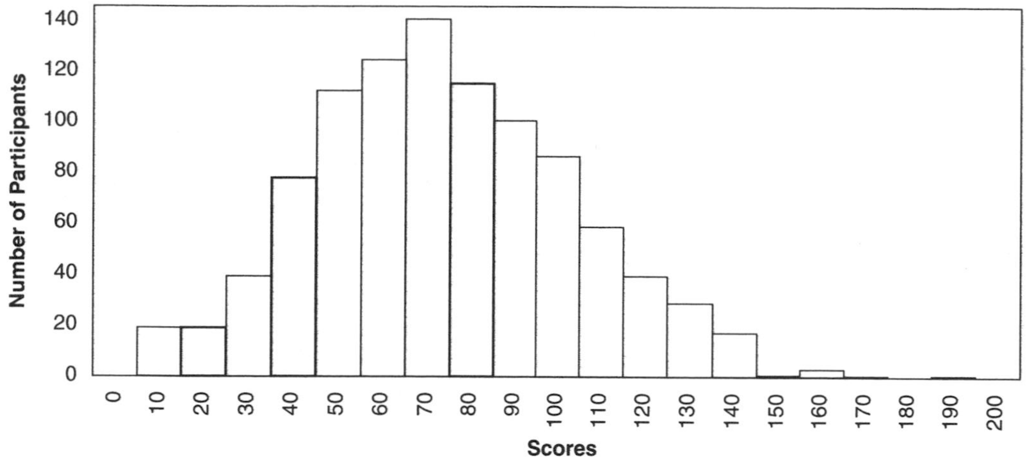

Note. SD = 29.96; M = 73.2; N = 946

art abilities, including some students with low-ability levels, most with mid-range-ability levels, and some obviously high-ability levels (see Figure 2).

Tasks on the TTC and CDAT measure different expectations, executions, product outcomes, completions, and scoring criteria. Nevertheless, correlation between these two tests was highly significant; a generalizability coefficient of .221 was obtained ($p = .0001$). This finding indicates that performance on the two tests is affected similarly by a factor, or factors, such as intelligence, problem-solving skills, or other abilities.

Distributions of scores on both the TTC and the CDAT indicate a skewness to the left consistent with what might be expected when assessing students in rural, underserved schools across the country. Students who lack exposure or experience with concepts and activities associated with any task should be expected to perform below normative standards because these often are established with urban and suburban populations who are experienced with a variety of arts resources in their schools and communities.

The TTC and CDAT measure differing sets of abilities. The TTC measures fluency, flexibility, and elaboration, commonly associated with the concept of creativity, and is based on both verbal and visual responses. The TTC appears to measure native, inherent abilities that are relatively unaffected by past experiences and skills. The CDAT measures both problem-solving skills and differential drawing abilities, as indicated by graphic responses to drawing tasks, but the scores are sensitive to past experiences and previously learned skills and techniques. CDAT scores, therefore, usually accelerate with age and instruction, whereas scores on the TTC remain relatively constant over time.

TTC, CDAT, and Achievement Test Scores. One important finding from this research was confirmation that, for third graders at each school, there was a positive correlation among scores on the TTC, CDAT, and state achievement tests. Although the correlation may not be as high as in more affluent, suburban communities, Clark and Zimmerman (1998) and others in the past (i.e., Hollingworth, 1926) and more recently (i.e., Pegnato & Birch, 1959; Yochim, 1967) often have speculated about a positive correlation between high intelligence and high abilities in the visual and performing arts. An interesting confirmation of that speculation was obtained in this study. Each of the three states cooperating with Project ARTS used a different, standardized achievement test as a measure of student performance. Students at the third grade with high scores on the CDAT and TTC as a group also had high scores on each of the local standardized achievement tests. In other words, students with high creativity scores and drawing ability scores also obtained substantially higher scores on language, mathematics, and reading tests in each of the three states. This consistency of results across all three states confirms that populations of high-achieving students in the visual arts also are high-achieving students in general (see Table 2).

TTC, CDAT, Achievement Tests, and Gender. Another important finding confirmed by this study is that gender performance for these rural students is relatively coequal on the TTC, CDAT, and achievement test subtests in Language, Mathematics, and Reading (see Tables 3 and 4). In elementary schools, generally, girls are expected to exceed boys in achievement scores and general school performance. No evidence was found to confirm this. The question is raised whether this expectation is based on more frequently measured and reported results from urban and suburban school populations, but not demonstrated in rural schools, where academic expectations and obligations for boys and girls may be relatively coequal. Certainly, differences between the performances of boys and girls on the TTC, CDAT, and achievement tests were not demonstrated in the rural schools cooperating with Project ARTS. The probability that male and female students are not substantially different in regard to the tests and tasks mentioned above is not consistent with values expressed in some of the rural communities participating in Project ARTS, as with the Indiana teacher who changed all of her peer nomination forms to require submission of both a girl's name and a boy's name on each item on forms used in her school. Her concern was that gender roles are established early in her community and clearly were reflected in her classroom. She reported that previous group selection and nomination procedures almost always resulted in single-sex groupings, although she had coequal expectations of performance for all of her students.

Similarly, performance on the Torrance Tests of Creativity and Clark's Drawing Abilities Test were not significantly different for boys and girls. This finding was consistent across the schools, except for one in South Carolina

Table 2   Correlations Between Art, Creativity, and Local Achievement Test Scores

	TTC	Language	Mathematics	Reading
Indiana				
CDAT	.3559* (105) p = .000	.2325* (104) p = .018	.2602* (104) p = .008	.3202* (104) p = .001
TTC		.2917* (99) p = .003	.4165* (99) p = .000	.3083* (99) p = .002
Language			.7142* (105) p = .000	.7026* (105) p = .000
Mathematics				.5928* (105) p = .000
New Mexico				
CDAT	.1238* (308) p = .030	.2971* (295) p = *.000	.2327* (303) p = .000	.2295* (304) p = .000
TTC		.1963* (293) p = .001	.1181* (303) p = .040	.1413* (303) p = .014
Language			.7369* (319) p = .000	.7462* (319) p = .000
Mathematics				.7016* (328) p = .000
South Carolina				
CDAT	.3259* (366) p = .000	.3244* (464) p = .000	.3239* (464) p = .000	.3198* (464) p = .000
TTC		.2642* (403) p = .000	.1677* (403) p = .001	.2539* (403) p = .000
Language			.6771* (523) p = .000	.7524* (523) p = .000
Mathematics				.6638* (523) p = .000

Note.* = < .05 significance level

Table 3   ANOVA Group Mean Comparisons of Achievement and Gender

ANOVA Group Mean Comparisons of Language Scores and Gender

Test	F	df	P-level
ISTEP (IN)	.9787	1.73	.5229
ITBS (CNM)	.0090	1.328	.9244
SAT-8 (SC)	2.3532	1.513	.1256

ANOVA Group Mean Comparisons of Mathematics Scores and Gender

Test	F	df	P-level
ISTEP (IN)	.6137	1.513	.4338
ITBS (NM)	1.6773	1.327	.1962
SAT-8 (SC)	1.4874	1.104	.2254

ANOVA Group Mean Comparisons of Reading Sores and Gender

Test	F	df	P-level
ISTEP (IN)	.5229	1.73	.5229
ITBS (NM)	.0090	1.328	.9244
SAT-8 (SC)	.1256	1.513	.1256

Table 4   TTC and CDAT Scores and Gender

Test	F	df	P-level
TTC (IN)	.2845	1.187	.5944
TTC (NM)	2.6185	1.342	.1065
TTC (SC)	.8813	1.476	.3483

ANOVA Group Mean Comparisons of CDAT Scores and Gender

Test	F	df	P-level
CDAT (IN)	1.8666	1.198	.1734
CDAT (NM)	2.2477	1.336	.1348
CDAT (SC)	13.4672	1.407	.0003

where girls scored higher than boys on most of the standardized test measures. This single exception may be a sampling error, given the relatively small number of students in each subgroup. On the other hand, it is consistent with the matriarchal character of the Gullah culture, in which women often play a dominant role in families and other social structures.

TTC, CDAT, Achievement Tests, and Age. Interestingly, performance for all third graders on the CDAT and TTC was not sensitive to the age of subjects. Neither the Torrance Tests of Creativity nor Clark's Drawing Abilities Test was significantly correlated with age of subjects (see Table 5). This may indicate that these tests are not sensitive to age differences in small incremental measures of time. The TTC and the CDAT, however, are sensitive to age across grades when divided into one-year incremental groups.

CONCLUSIONS AND RECOMMENDATIONS

The import of developing identification procedures in Project ARTS indicates that artistically talented students can be found in almost any school, anywhere in the country. Identifying artistically talented students in rural communities may require "bending the rules" in atypical situations and having local community groups, in cooperation with local teachers, develop instruments to identify high-ability students (Fredette, 1993; Smutny, 1997). In Project ARTS, this often was accomplished with unconventional instruments and procedures. Fortunately, we had enough staff well acquainted with identification problems to support the teachers in Indiana, New Mexico, and South Carolina. Some students entered these programs who may not have been correctly identified, but being open about procedures offered many high-potential or high-ability students opportunities they may never have experienced. The atypical measures used often lacked standardization because they were locally designed and untested except on local populations. Many of these local procedures proved to be appropriate when used in conjunction with other locally designed procedures. The most difficult step was to convince teachers to respect the potential and abilities of their students and have faith in their own abilities to recognize those with talents.

Data reported for TTC, CDAT, and achievement test scores have implications for the identification of artistically talented students from ethnically diverse, rural, underserved, economically challenged communities. The CDAT has high correlations with the TTC used in this research, although the TTC was a modified instrument and may not be appropriate as an identification procedure for school testing. We, therefore, recommend using the CDAT as a measure for identification of students with high potential or high abilities in the visual arts. If the CDAT is used as an identification measure, boys and girls of different ages within the same grade can be identified to participate in an enrichment program according to their CDAT scores, without reference to sex or age. It should be noted that many elementary teachers claim that the arts offer students who are not academically able opportunities to achieve that are not available to them in other school subjects. On the other hand, data in this study indicate that genuinely high achievement in the visual arts is most likely to be accomplished by students who are generally high achieving in other school subjects.

Table 5 Regression and Analysis of Variance of Torrance Tests of Creativity, Clark's Drawing Abilities Test, and Birth Month of Subjects

Source	df	Sum of Squares	Mean Squares	F ratio
Torrance Tests of Creativity				
Regression	1	406.7822	406.7822	.45116
Residual	901	812368.9309	901.6303	
Clark's Drawing Abilities Test				
Regression	1	79.0270	79.0270	.3346
Residual	1016	7171.98767	7.0590	

We also recommend that a number of different measures (several local measures, the CDAT, and achievement test scores) be used in programs that have similar populations to those in Project ARTS. In the future, more research should be conducted to see whether recommendations from Project ARTS about identification procedures are applicable to other contexts with different populations. As a result of identification procedures used in this project, it is hoped that generalities about identification of visual arts students from diverse backgrounds will form a research base from which other communities will be able to develop programs for different populations of high-ability students with interests, potential, and advanced abilities in the visual arts.

REFERENCES

Anastasi, A. (1988). *Psychological testing* (6th ed.). New York: Macmillan.

Bachtel, A. E. (1988). *A study of current selection and identification processes and schooling for K-12 artistically gifted and talented students* (Doctoral Dissertation, University of Southern California). Dissertation Abstracts International, 49, 12A-3597

Baldwin, A. (1984). *The Baldwin Identification Matrix 2 for Identification of Gifted and Talented.* New York: Trillium Press.

Bolster, S. J. (1990, March). *Collaboration on curriculum.* Paper presented at the Rural Education Symposium of the American Council on Rural Special Education and the National Rural and Small Schools Consortium, Tucson, AZ.

Brooks, P. R. (1997). Targeting potentially talented and gifted minority students for academic advancement. In J. F. Smutny (Ed.), *The young gifted child* (pp. 133–146). Cresskill, NJ: Hampton.

Buros, O. (Ed.). (1972). *The seventh mental measurements yearbook.* Highland Park, NJ: The Gryphon Press.

Clark, G. (1989). Screening and identifying students talented in the visual arts: Clark's Drawing Abilities Test. *Gifted Child Quarterly, 33*(3), 98–105.

Clark, G. (1992). Using history to design current research: The background of Clark's Drawing Abilities Test. In P. Amburgy, D. Soucy, M. Stankiewicz, B. Wilson, & M. Wilson (Eds.), *The history of art education: Proceedings from the second Penn State conference,* 1989 (pp. 191–199). Reston, VA: National Art Education Association (NAEA).

Clark, G. (1993). Judging children's drawings as measures of art abilities. *Studies in Art Education, 34,* 72–81.

Clark, G., & Wilson, T. (1991). Screening and identifying gifted/talented students in the visual arts with Clark's Drawing Abilities Test. *Roeper Review, 13,* 92–97.

Clark, G., & Zimmerman, E. (1992). *Issues and practices related to identification of gifted and talented students in the visual arts.* (Research Monograph No. 9202). Storrs, CT: The National Research Center on the Gifted and Talented.

Clark, G., & Zimmerman, E. (1994). *Programming opportunities for students talented in the visual arts.* (Research Monograph No. RBDM 9402). Storrs, CT: The National Research Center on the Gifted and Talented.

Clark, G., & Zimmerman, E. (1998). Nurturing the arts in programs for gifted and talented students. *Phi Delta Kappan, 79,* 747–756.

Eisner, E. W. (1972). *Educating artistic vision.* New York: Macmillan.

Elam, A. H., Goodwin, N., & Doughty, R. (1988). *Guidelines for the identification of artistically gifted and talented students* (Revised). Columbia, SC: South Carolina State Department of Education. (ERIC Document Reproduction Service No. ED 306761).

Fredette, B. (1993). *Issues in identifying visually gifted young children.* (ERIC Document Reproduction Service, No. ED370568)

Freeman, J. (1991). *Gifted children growing up.* London: Cassell.

Hamblen, K. (1988). If it will be tested, it will be taught. A rationale worthy of examination. *Art Education, 41*(5), 59–62.

Hollingworth, L. S. (1926). *Gifted children: Their nature and nurture.* New York: Macmillan.

Keirouz, K. S. (1990). *The Indiana guide on identification of gifted/talented students.* Indianapolis, IN: Indiana Department of Education.

Leonhard, C. (1991). *The status of arts education in American public schools: Report on a survey conducted by the National Arts Education Research Center at the University of Illinois.* Urbana-Champaign, IL: Council for Research in Music Education, University of Illinois.

Linn, L. L., & Gronlund, N. E. (1995). *Measurement and assessment in teaching* (7th ed.). Englewood Cliffs, NJ: Merrill.

Nachtigal, P. N. (1992). Rural schools: Obsolete . . . or harbinger of the future? *Educational Horizons, 70,* 66–70.

Pegnato, C. W., & Birch, J. (1959). Locating gifted children in junior high schools: A comparison of methods. *Exceptional Children, 25,* 300–304.

Sabol, F. R. (1994). *A critical examination of visual arts achievement tests from state departments of education in the United States.* Unpublished doctoral dissertation, Indiana University, Bloomington, IN.

Smutny, J. F. (1997). Special opportunities: Challenges and opportunities. In J. F. Smutny (Ed.), *The young gifted child* (pp. 91–94). Cresskill, NJ: Hampton.

Spicker, H. H., Southern, W. T., & Davis, B. I. (1987). The rural gifted child. *Gifted Child Quarterly, 31,* 155–157.

Swassing, R. H. (1985). *Teaching gifted children and adolescents.* Columbus, OH: Merrill.

Torrance, E. P. (1997). Talent among children who are economically disadvantaged or culturally different. In J. F. Smutny (Ed.), *The gifted young child* (pp. 95–118). Cresskill, NJ: Hampton.

VanTassel-Baska, J. (1988). *Comprehensive curriculum for gifted learners.* Denver, CO: Love.

VanTassel-Baska, J. (Ed.). (1998). *Excellence in educating gifted and talented learners* (3rd ed.). Denver, CO: Love.

Yochim, L. D. (1967). *Perceptual growth in creativity.* Scranton, PA: International Textbook.

Zimmerman, E. (1992). Assessing students' progress and achievements in art. *Art Education, 45*(6), 34–38

Zimmerman, E. (1994). How should students' progress and achievements be assessed? A case for assessment that is responsive to diverse students' needs. *Visual Arts Research, 20*(1), 29–35.

7

Views of Self, Family Background, and School: Interviews With Artistically Talented Students

Gilbert A. Clark

Enid Zimmerman

Indiana University

Twenty IU Summer Arts Institute students, ages 13 through 17, were interviewed to learn more about their perceptions of their early art talent, adult and peer encouragement, position in their families, future expectations, interest in drawing, living environments, familiarity with artists,

Editor's Note: From Clark, G. A., & Zimmerman, E. (1988). Views of self, family background, and school: Interviews with artistically talented students. *Gifted Child Quarterly*, 32(4), 340-346. © 1988 National Association for Gifted Children. Reprinted with permission.

schooling, and art ability. Results of these interviews were compared with findings by Getzels and Csikszentmihalyi, Bloom, Chetelat, Taylor, and Guskin, Zimmerman, Okolo, and Peng. Similarities and differences were found between results of this study and findings by these researchers.

Although information is available about characteristics of students talented in the visual arts, the findings are confusing because they have been generated at various periods of time, reflect differing methodologies, and emphasize divergent research questions. Researchers need to resolve the inconsistencies and contradictions that emerged from past inquiry about artistically talented students and create a body of research comparable to that which exists about academically gifted students (Clark and Zimmerman, 1984).

Researchers in psychology and art education have conducted interviews with young art students or artists in the early years of their careers to gain access to their personal reminiscences. Getzels and Csikszentmihalyi (1976) interviewed young artists when they were college art students and after they left school. Retrospective accounts reported in this research were closer in time to actual events and therefore, the researchers claimed, less subject to distortion than most biographical accounts. From these interviews, Getzels and Csikszentmihalyi hoped to construct a pattern of socialization into art and answer questions about how a person becomes an artist and a creative problem finder. Bloom (1985) and his associates, through interviews with subjects, siblings, and parents, examined processes by which individuals reach high levels of accomplishment in their fields before the age of 35. Their subjects included two art groups, concert pianists and sculptors, as well as high achievers in science, mathematics, and sports. They felt the information they needed about developing talent in young people could be secured through the retrospective accounts of people who had already achieved high levels of capability in selected fields.

A few researchers have interviewed young artistically talented students to gain information about their perceptions and life situations. Chetelat (1982) interviewed six artistically talented students, aged 11 to 14, to discern differences and similarities of specific characteristics and the living and learning environments between these students and the early childhood experiences of six eminent artists as recorded in autobiographical accounts. Using interviews and open-ended questionnaires, Guskin, Zimmerman, Okolo, and Peng (1986) studied artistically talented and academically gifted students, aged 9 to 15, in order to understand how gifted students view themselves and how they interpret their giftedness. Taylor (1986), drawing extensively upon Hargreaves' (1982) work with adults, interviewed artistically talented students in England, ages 14 to 18, to determine how they developed a commitment to one or more art forms and how they identified or empathized with art objects.

RESEARCH QUESTIONS

The recent use of interviews by researchers in psychology and art education to study perceptions and life situations of artistically talented students has suggested research questions that can be applied to talented art students in a variety of settings. Interview questions are categorized into topics concerned with early art talent, adult and peer encouragement, position in the family, future expectations, early interest in reading and looking at books, interest in drawing, living environments, familiarity with artists, schooling, and perceptions of art ability. These categories were addressed in the present study in an effort to gain more information about the characteristics of artistically talented students described in the literature cited above. Although the Bloom (1985) study involved accomplished professionals and Getzel's and Csikszentmihalyi's subjects were college age students, it was hypothesized that reminiscences of these populations, compared with the population in the present study, would probably differ in degree and intensity but not in kind. This speculation will be explored further in subsequent studies.

Putting the Research to Use

There are many popular misconceptions about characteristics and abilities of students talented in art. Some of these misconceptions underlie problems relative to identifying, educating, and providing services for artistically talented students. Of particular interest are the views of self, family background, and education expressed by the artistically talented students who were interviewed in this study. Research of the type reported can lead to creation of a structure for understanding artistically talented students as a specific population within schools. Teachers, counselors, and others who work with artistically talented students need to be aware of and understand how this population differs from others in order to create programs that will best meet the educational, emotional, and social needs of such students.

Results of this pilot study will be compared with findings of all researchers cited in order to expand available knowledge and create a foundation for future research that may lead ultimately to creation of structures for understanding artistically talented students as a specific population. Teachers and others who work with artistically talented students need to understand how this population differs from other students in order to identify them, provide services, and best meet their educational needs.

METHODOLOGY

Subjects

The Indiana University Summer Arts Institute, a residential two-week program for students talented in the visual arts, was the setting for this study. Participants were 20 students attending the Institute in 1986 and 1987 who were nominated by art teachers or other school personnel as artistically talented, based upon criteria developed by the Institute staff. These students were entering grades 7 through 11 in the following fall semester with a mean grade of 9.9. They ranged from 13 through 17 years of age with a mean age of 14 years and 9 months. In 1986, 11 of 62 students (18%) and in 1987, nine of 50 students (18%) were interviewed. Of the 20 students interviewed 12 were females (60%) and eight were males (40%). The overall percentage of male and female participants in 1986 and 1987 was nearly 50% males and 50% females.

The majority of students who attended the Institute in 1986 and 1987 were from Indiana; five were from out of state, three were from other countries, and seven had been born in other countries and had been living in the United States for less than three years. Eight of the students interviewed were from other countries or had been born outside the United States and had been living in the United States for less than three years. These students represented 9% of the total population of 112. Countries in which these students were born included Brazil, Korea, Malaysia, New Zealand, Singapore, Spain, Taiwan, and Viet Nam. About one third of the students attending the Institute in 1986 and 1987 received some form of financial aid; this same percentage was true for the students who were interviewed.

Residence

Of the 12 students interviewed from the United States, eight were from communities with less than 50,000 people, two were from communities with between 50,000 and 100,000 people, and two were from a large city with a population of over 100,000. All the international students were from capitals or other large cities in their home countries.

Parents' Occupations

Thirty-five parents were reported by the 20 students interviewed. As indicated on application forms, subjects' parents were reported to be working in the following U.S. Census (1987) categories of occupations (the number of parents within each category is given in parentheses): Executive, Administrative, Managerial

(3), Professional, Specialty (7), Sales (5), Administrative Support Operations (4), Precision Production, Craft, Repair (2), Operations, Fabricators, Laborers (2), and Service (2). Occupations reported for ten parents do not occur in the U.S. Census occupational categories: Housewife (7), Student (2), and Retiree (1).

Parents' occupations were widely distributed across the categories of occupations reported for the 1987 U.S. Census. There were nearly as many mothers as fathers working in each of the occupational categories across the entire scale. Of the ten parents whose description does not occur on the census list of occupations, seven were housewives (20%). Seven (20%) of the female parents, however, were employed in the executive, professional, and sales categories.

Siblings

The number of children in the families of students interviewed ranged from 1 to 14, with 6.92 the average number of children in each family. This figure is skewed because three students came from families with 7, 11, or 14 children. The majority of students (14) came from families of one to three children; only one student was an only child. A large number (80%) of the students were the oldest or youngest child in their families.

Data Collection

According to Brenner, Brown, and Canter (1985), the strength of the interview technique is that both the interviewer and the person being interviewed can explore meanings of relevant questions and this procedure can produce immediate answers. Although reliability and validity of data collected through interviews as well as methods of data analysis have been questioned, Brenner (1985) contended that interview techniques used in research need not bias the process of data collection and analysis and can support interactions that take place so that the person interviewed reports adequately and honestly. As suggested by Brenner, in this study a problem was identified, other writings related to the problem were studied, and an interview guideline was finalized.

Interviews for this study were conducted by the two co-directors of the Institute during the first week of the Institute in out-of-class time. Each director interviewed five male and five female students. Interviews, which lasted from 1½ to 2 hours, were tape recorded and later transcribed by a person trained for this task. Because the interviewers were interested in investigating similarities and differences between artistically talented international students and talented students from the United States, one third of the students selected to be interviewed were born outside the U.S. (although they represented only 9% of the total Institute population). Students from the United States were chosen by random selection. All students selected were asked for voluntary participation and, in a few instances, some declined to be interviewed.

An interview protocol (available from the authors) containing nine major categories and three to six questions within each category was used. The nine interview categories and related questions were adapted from research done by Getzels and Csikszentmihalyi (1976), Chetelat (1982), Bloom (1985), Guskin et al. (1986), and Taylor (1986). This protocol was used to guide interviews, but student responses determined the course of interview dialogue. All categories were covered with each subject but not necessarily in the same order and not all subjects responded to every question.

Data Analysis

Content analysis, as described by Mostyn (1985), has been used extensively to analyze "unstructured, open-ended research material" that results from "nondirective questions which, by their nature, impose as few constraints on respondent's answers as possible" (p. 115). In qualitative research, Mostyn contends, the sample is small, interviews usually last more than one hour, respondents react to questions that are structured within a general framework, the objective is to expand the knowledge base gained by previous data; results are analyzed by content analysis, and the final report is based on understanding attitudes and behaviors of respondents.

According to Holsti (1969), content analysis as a means for analyzing data meets the requirements of *objectivity*, in terms of carrying out each step according to stipulated rules, *inclusion and exclusion* of categories according to systematically applied rules, and *generalizeability* of findings that have some theoretical relevance. Gordon (1978) described the content analysis process as steps in which the researcher listens and reads collected data critically, tries to discover meaning in the data, looks for significant relationships, synthesizes, and arrives at conclusions based on the data.

In this study, following recommendations made by Holsti (1969), Gordon (1978), and Mostyn (1985), transcriptions of all interviews were coded by one of the investigators. Each relevant idea found in subjects' responses was recorded in their own words on 3" × 5" index cards and coded appropriately. These cards then were sorted according to similar themes by both investigators. When five or six cards accumulated as a theme, a rule that described the conditions for these assignments was established and a rule card was created. Rules were rewritten as more cards were assigned to each group, and cards were moved from one group to another to fit emerging rules. Larger categories were formed with subcategories of related rules. These new categories were derived from the data and were not necessarily formed to correspond to categories or questions in the original interview protocol.

RESULTS

Large categories resulting from analysis of the interview data were labelled (1) views of self, (2) views of family and home environment, (3) views of school and studying art, and (4) views of teachers, students, curriculum and setting at the

IU Summer Arts Institute. These categories, with subcategories and representative examples of direct quotations from students, are described as follows.

VIEWS OF SELF

Past Remembrances

- Most students remembered becoming interested in art at a pre-school or primary school level.
- Some students remembered doing fantasy drawings when they were young, others remembered doing realistic drawings.
- Many students were aware that they were superior to other children in art.

> "When I was younger, I liked to sketch . . . Ever since I remember I was drawing, but the earliest picture I remember was when I was four . . . It's in three or four sections and it's got like home and a hell place and a heaven place."

- Most students remembered specific people and incidents as triggers to when they first became interested in art.

> "My father has a friend, he was an artist, he for one of my birthdays or something . . . made a book for me. I was one of the characters with my friends. It was really good. I would just stare at this thing forever, it was so good. I drew a lot from that."

Present Interest

- Girls, more than boys, reported beginning with an emotional need and then learning skills to help them express themselves in art. Boys, more than girls, stated a concern for developing technical skills and did not report creating art for expressive reasons.

> "When I draw I look at the thing, I concentrate on it, look at the different outlines, the shape of it, think about what it's like, how it looks good in different positions, and then I start to draw it."
>
> "When you are happy, and when you are upset, I always draw mostly black. I mean the color's usually dark and dreary and everything. You can see the expression like how Picasso drew animals . . . It's kind of weird."

- Both boys and girls reported their favorite subject matter as observed objects, places they'd been, landscapes, human figures, and fantasy figures.
- The most commonly used medium reported was pencil because it is the medium with which they have the most experience and it is inexpensive and available.
- Five students indicated they like to draw realistically; they do not copy, but use illustrations as sources of inspiration. Five other students mentioned

that they copied from comics when they were young but now look at illustrations for ideas.

> "When I'm drawing my own characters and stuff I go in my closet because I've got a lot of books and I just get out a couple and I like to take bits and pieces off every character to create my own character."

– A majority of students felt good about themselves and their abilities and could accept criticism in order to improve their art work.

> "I don't mind being criticized. It's like you've got to accept it, you can't go through life thinking that you're doing everything right. I'm sure everybody has a lot of mistakes, I'm fifteen years old, and I've still got a lot to learn."

– Some students expressed interest in working alone while others needed to work with others to function optimally.
– Five students felt that artists look at things differently; they see more than others see and need skill, imagination, and talent to paint.

> "I think artists can look at things better, are better observers than other people. They can really look at things instead of just passing it over I mean an artist might see something that someone else might not."

– Most students were able to name a favorite artist. Artists named were well known ones such as Matisse, Picasso, DaVinci, and Dali. Most students said they did not learn about artists in school.

Future Expectations

– Half the students expressed an interest in having a career in the arts either as cartoonists, painters, teachers, interior decorators, or in advertising. More girls than boys wanted to be artists, although three girls mentioned pressure from their family to marry and raise a family and view their art only as an avocation.

> "Ever since I was small I always knew what I was going to be, always an artist . . . You know when other kids say I want to be an astronaut, well I always want to be an artist, and the parents would look at me like, you know, this kid's been watching too many movies."

VIEWS OF FAMILY AND HOME ENVIRONMENT

Family and Friends

– Most students (70%) reported that they were encouraged in their art work by their mother, father, or both. Fifteen percent of the students noted that family members other than their parents encouraged them but did not mention their parents. Three students (15%) reported that no members of their family encouraged or supported their interest in art work. No differences were noted between boys and girls in these findings.

- Only three parents and one sibling were reported as having studied art or doing art work as a hobby. Of these, two parents were in one family.

- Ten students (50%) mentioned that none of their friends were interested in art; five (25%) did note that they had one or more friends who were interested in art.

Home Environment

- Thirteen students (65%) reported that they had a place to do art work in their homes; the remaining seven (35%) did not. Those who reported working in their home did not have special studio-like facilities.

  > "When I work at home I work in my bedroom. Away from everybody. I like to be quiet and get away from everything. I just lie on the floor or my bed or whatever to draw."

- Of 18 who responded, 12 (60%) remembered having illustrated books (comics or wildlife books) in their homes. Only two students (10%) reported having any art books in their homes.

  > "Just every time we'd go to the grocery store my mother would buy me one of the little books and we'd read them. They always had pictures on every page."

- Students from the U.S. tended to have stayed in a local area and not to have traveled beyond their home state. Most international students mentioned having moved a number of times and had traveled to one or more other countries.

  > "I've traveled but I mean only to places like we went to go see our cousins in North Carolina, but the places I really want to see are Chicago, New York City, and Manhattan."

VIEWS OF SCHOOL AND STUDYING ART

School

- Many students from rural areas said that school offered them their only access to a social community.

  > "The first semester of school is when I really like it. I enjoy seeing my friends. I live out in the country . . . I bus into school and in the summer I don't really get to see my friends."

- Most, however, mentioned difficulty in finding friends at school who shared common interests in the arts.

"I don't really have a group I can relate to in school . . . I went to a really small school before I went to high school and I really haven't found any people that I run around with or anything."

– Seventy-five percent (15) of the students took art classes in their regular schools; 25% (5) reported that they didn't have time to take art classes in or out of school due to the pressure to complete an academic curriculum.

"I don't take art right now in high school, but I used to . . . it's an elective class and I have to take foreign language. That's the only reason I'm not taking it."

– Twelve students reported taking arts-related classes outside school. Eight took visual arts classes, and four were enrolled in performing arts classes. An equal number of these were boys and girls.
– International students enrolled in outside art classes tended to take private lessons with a particular teacher, with an emphasis upon developing skills and techniques. U.S. students in outside classes tended to attend group lessons at a university or museum, with emphasis upon creative self-expression. U.S. students also attended many different types of arts classes.
– Nearly half of the students mentioned the impact of winning awards as helping to maintain their interest in art and contributing to support from their families.

"After my paintings started winning in the art show my mother started looking for teachers to teach me because I wanted to paint."

– Negative aspects of awards also were mentioned, including (1) the effect of perpetuating adherence to a rewarded style, (2) creation of tension between winners and non-winners, and (3) lack of understanding or awareness of how competitions were judged and how winners were chosen.

"I did get the ribbons and so I'd think about the past things I've done before, that type of thing, that's what I'd usually draw."

– All students reported receiving good grades. Subjects they liked most were science, English, history, and mathematics. A few international students mentioned that they disliked studying English. Typical reports of grades were high, including mostly As and Bs. There were no differences between boys and girls in their grades and preferences.

I'm interested in art and biology. I was thinking it would be nice to combine the two. I like the cells of animals and things like that and it's really interesting to me."
"I have a 4.0 average in school. I like history, that's my favorite and algebra because I like working with figures and stuff—I like them all."

Studying Art

– Three images of regular art teachers emerged. One was supportive, but not challenging students to higher levels of achievement. Another was challenging, but failing to reinforce or support accomplishments. The third was challenging, but not offering instruction about how to succeed.

> "I get sick of being told everything I do is good . . . I know it's not perfect but she's like 'it's great'! I'm going 'do you really'? . . . But it's like 'it's great, don't do anything more', and I never get satisfied with my work." "I work hard and everything and I think I'm doing my best and she'll always tell me that I could do better, but she won't tell me how."

– Students who had lived in other countries, as compared to those in the U.S., reported their art classes tended to be more crowded, were taught more formally with an emphasis on techniques, were based upon specific assignments from workbooks, and were stricter and more rigorous. They also reported that they had to pass examinations in both art and art history.

VIEWS OF TEACHERS, STUDENTS, AND CURRICULUM AND SETTING AT THE INSTITUTE

Teachers

– Most students found that teachers at the Institute (1) challenged them more than those in their regular schools, (2) taught them to use new media, (3) made them think about what they were doing and consider new ways of looking at things, (4) made them look more carefully and accurately, and (5) taught them to consider how to express themselves through careful use of techniques.

> "I couldn't draw—the second he (Institute teacher) explained it to me I knew what I had been doing wrong. He said that I was looking at it as what it is and my brain was drawing what it knows it looks like. Once I learned that I started looking at it as a shape and then my drawing got one hundred percent better. No comparison."

Students

– The majority of students expressed pleasure at being grouped with others with similar interests and abilities.

> "It's fun to be here because there's a lot of people . . . who think like us, 'cause in school they're not really interested at this point in life, not a lot of people are interested in art."

- Most students enjoyed working at a high level of difficulty, felt that they were doing better work than in their regular classrooms, and realized how much they learned in a short period of time.
- Many students expressed pleasure at the openness of conversations outside classes in which they shared ideas and critiqued each others' art work.

> "One thing, in class we enjoy ourselves; we enjoy ourselves so much that we want to work . . . like we enjoy, we talk, we joke; I feel if I enjoy myself I can do more work and my work will come out better and better."

A number of students expressed awareness of having learned a lot about themselves both socially and through learning new techniques and means of expression.

> "Sometimes when we've been standing up and drawing for two hours straight and that's kind of tiring and everybody gets all edgy . . . later on before you go to sleep you sit down and think about it and it's all clear."

- Most students reported that they were surrounded by other students of comparable or superior abilities and that they had to work hard to do well in relation to what the teachers expected of them and others.
- A few students expressed awareness of their reluctance to abandon their own style or change their approach to creating art because they had been rewarded for these things in the past.

> "The Institute is not as good as I hoped . . . it's the painting . . . I'm not used to painting this way . . . but I came here to learn new things and so I'm learning new things . . . I like my own style and I don't want a different style forced on me."

Curriculum and Setting

- Most students mentioned that smaller Institute classes encouraged better communication and instruction.

> "In my class there are only thirteen . . . we can really move and talk more . . . we can really be more of a group . . . if there's really a big group, you can't get to know everybody."

New experiences for most students, such as going to an art museum, hearing a lecture by an art historian, or visiting an art store, were mentioned as memorable Institute events.

> "I enjoyed just everything, really. Going to the art store—that's the first time I've ever been into a real art shop. Then going to the artist's studio . . . that was real, an interesting experience."

DISCUSSION AND CONCLUSIONS

Views of Self

In this study most students were found to be aware of their art talent, interested in improving their abilities, and introspective about the role of art in their lives. Many students were aware that they possessed unusual interest and ability in the arts, a finding similar to those reported by Chetelat (1982) and Bloom (1985). Students at the Institute had favorable views of themselves and gifted and talented students in general, as did subjects in the Guskin, et al. (1986) study. Chetelat (1982) and Bloom (1985) also found, as did this study, that young people with talent in the arts find art making experiences rewarding. Although Getzels and Csikszentmihalyi (1976) reported that emotional crises were stimulants to creating art, the majority of subjects in this study made no reference to an emotional crisis as the basis of their art making. Rather, they spoke about art making stimulated by pleasurable experiences. Students in this study did not indicate that they were using art for emotional release. More girls than boys, however, described their art making as a means of self expression rather than building techniques and skills.

Four other findings by Getzels and Csikszentmihalyi (1976) were similar to findings in this study: (1) young people who are talented in art draw many of the same images, such as cartoons and comic book heroes, as other similarly aged students, (2) their drawings were praised more than those of other students in their classes, (3) they devoted a great deal of time and energy to drawing, and (4) they remember drawing from ages six to eight. Findings in this study are not consistent with those of Chetelat (1982), who found a high degree of solitary art making among his subjects. Institute students were divided almost equally between favoring solitary work and working in groups.

Views of Family and Home Environment

In this study most students' family members encouraged them to maintain their interest in art although they did not have art backgrounds or travel extensively. Few students had friends interested in art, yet they continued to maintain their participation in art. Chetelat (1982) and Bloom (1985) reported strong support from both parents and encouragement for their subjects. Subjects of this study reported similar support in most cases. This finding contradicts the report of Getzels and Csikszentmihalyi (1976) that young art students frequently received support only from their mothers and had harsh memories of their fathers.

Bloom (1985) reported that parents of talented individuals varied greatly in the level of education they had completed, the type of work they engaged in, their economic level, and their avocational interests and activities. In this study students' responses and application form data verified a similar finding about parents' occupations. One aspect of the findings of this study, however, contradicts

Bloom's description of modelling by parents. Bloom reports homes that emphasized music and the arts. Few subjects in this study were offered such opportunities either at home or in any other aspect of their social lives.

Chetelat (1962) reported that all his subjects showed "a great interest in viewing books at an early age" (p. 95) and were stimulated by book illustrations. Subjects of this study recalled having read illustrated books, but few reported a relationship between their recollection of book illustrations and their own drawing, except for comic books.

Views of School and Studying Art

Most students in this study reported that school offered a social community but that they did not have many friends with similar interests. Many of them took art classes outside school and had won awards which they perceived as having both positive and negative effects. Almost all were good students who earned high grades and enjoyed school. Their art teachers were recalled as having encouraged or challenged them, but they often expressed a need for more rigorous and supportive instruction.

Recollections of their art teachers varied widely among subjects in this study although many did recall specific teachers who had rewarded and encouraged them. Unlike Chetelat's (1982) subjects, not all subjects recalled their art teachers positively. That selecting students to exhibit their art or participate in an art club or praising them for specific achievements served to motivate and encourage them to continue to make art was found to be true in this study as well as in studies by Chetelat (1982) and Bloom (1985).

Unlike subjects in Getzels and Csikszentmihalyi's (1976) study, all of the subjects in this study reported positive reactions to their schooling and were, by and large, excellent students in most subjects. Recollections of art teachers agreed with Bloom's (1985) descriptions of early, elementary school teachers as child-oriented, using approval and praise and making early learning pleasant and rewarding. Institute students perceived their need both to be challenged and to be taught higher level abilities that would improve their art work. In this, they are anticipating their need for advanced teachers who are professional, experienced with highly talented students, and who will demand high achievement and commitment to their talent area. These are what Bloom has described as middle level teachers who are important in the development of talent in the arts.

VIEWS OF TEACHER, STUDENTS, AND CURRICULUM AND SETTING

Students recognized major differences between classes at the Institute and their regular classes; they were pleased to be grouped with others like themselves. They became more conscious and critical of their own abilities and took advantage of the many university facilities available to them at the Institute.

Taylor (1986) described students talented in art as having "illuminating experiences" that changed their lives through encounters with original works of art. In this study similar but less intense experiences at the Institute were reported by students who had never previously visited an art museum, attended a concert, or visited an artist's studio.

Analysis of the findings from this study has verified or called into question the results of previous research about artistically talented students. More research needs to be conducted through interview techniques with more subjects in diverse settings to elucidate further our understanding of perceptions and life situations of artistically talented students.

REFERENCES

Bloom, B. S. (Ed.) (1985). *Developing talent in young people.* New York: Ballantine.

Brenner, M. (1985). Intensive interviewing. In M. Brenner, J. Brown, & D. Canter (Eds.), *The research interview: Uses and approaches* (pp. 147–162). London: Academic Press.

Brenner, M., Brown, J., & Canter, D. (1985). Introduction. In M. Brenner, J. Brown, & D. Canter (Eds.), *The research interview: Uses and approaches* (pp. 1–8). London: Academic Press.

Chetelat, F. J. (1982). A preliminary investigation into the life situations and environments which nurture the artistically gifted and talented child. *Dissertation Abstracts International, 43*(10), 3190 A. (University Microfilms No. DA 830 5624).

Clark, G., & Zimmerman, E. (1984). *Educating artistically talented students.* Syracuse, NY: Syracuse University Press.

Getzels, J., & Csikszentmihalyi, M. (1976). *The creative vision: A longitudinal study of problem finding in art.* New York: John Wiley and Sons.

Gordon, W. I. (1978). *Communication: Personal and public.* New York: Alfred.

Guskin, S. L., Zimmerman, E., Okolo, C., & Peng, C.-Y. J. (1986). Being labeled gifted or talented: Meanings and effects perceived by students in special programs. *Gifted Child Quarterly, 30*(2), 61–65.

Hargreaves, D. (1982). *The challenge for the comprehensive school.* London: Routledge and Kegan Paul.

Holsti, O. R. (1969). *Content analysis for the social sciences and humanities.* Reading, MA: Addison.

Mostyn, B. (1985). The content analysis of qualitative research data: A dynamic approach. In M. Brenner, J. Brown, & D. Canter (Eds.), *The research interview: Uses and approaches* (pp. 115–145). London: Academic Press.

Taylor, R. (1986). *Educating for art.* London: Longman.

US Department of Commerce Bureau of Census. (1987). *Statistical abstract of the United States* (Publication No. 107 Ed). Washington, DC: US Bureau of Census.

8

I Don't Want to Sit in the Corner Cutting Out Valentines: Leadership Roles for Teachers of Talented Art Students

Enid Zimmerman

Indiana University

Two research studies which focus on the process and results of educating teachers of high ability visual arts students to take leadership roles in their schools, communities, and beyond are presented. One study involved focus groups of 1994 participants in the Artistically Talented Program (ATP) at Indiana University; the other included a survey sent to all teachers who participated in ATP from 1991 to 1995. A framework based on a content analysis of the data in these two studies has applicability to other

Editor's Note: From Zimmerman, E. (1997). I don't want to sit in the corner cutting out valentines: Leadership roles for teachers of talented art students. *Gifted Child Quarterly*, 41(1), 33-41. © 1997 National Association for Gifted Children. Reprinted with permission.

inservice education programs for teachers of talented art students. Knowledge of subject matter content, pedagogy, building self-esteem, and allowing choices can lead teachers of artistically talented students, who have leadership potential, to collaborate with others. Teachers can become empowered to make changes in their private and professional lives that eventually result in communities of caring professionals able to assume leadership roles.

E ducating teachers to become empowered and take leadership roles in a variety of educational communities is a growing issue in contemporary educational practice. Because most teachers in the United States are women, except in higher education, we need to encourage and educate women, who are interested and who have potential, to become teacher/leaders (Thurber & Zimmerman, 1996; Zimmerman, in press). It is important to form communities of teachers who take educational leadership roles in their own classrooms as well as to form contexts in which communal relationships are valued (Lieberman & McLaughlin, 1992). It is also important to establish communities of teachers who have opportunities to engage in collaborative efforts and build networks that lead to conducting inquiry into professional practices (Darling-Hammond, 1993). Inservice teacher educators should help classroom teachers gain confidence in speaking out, developing a sense of agency, becoming challengers, taking initiatives, and determining what and how to teach in their own classrooms (Sprague, 1992). According to Sprague, through collaboration and shared leadership, teachers can be empowered to social and political activism and thus become professionals who are influential and valuable to society.

Maeroff (1988) studied national inservice teacher education programs in math, science, and humanities education and concluded that these programs have potential to build leadership by breaking down isolation and building networks among teachers, thereby bolstering their confidence, increasing their knowledge of subject matter and pedagogy, and involving them in projects in which they have access to decision making. In the most successful programs Maeroff (1988) studied, teachers were paid to spend time in intense summer sessions, and their learning was reinforced throughout the school year. Teachers who attended these programs bonded and continued relationships with other teachers in the program after the formal inservice ended.

Although research about inservice art teachers has increased in recent years (Galbraith, 1995; Zimmerman, 1994), there still is little inquiry, particularly in staff development aimed at developing leadership roles in art education. The following two related studies were motivated by my interest in discovering whether inservice teachers, studying in a summer program at Indiana University, were able to build community relationships through networking, to take initiatives to change their classroom practice, to engage actively in the content of their disciplines, and eventually to become leaders in their schools, communities, and beyond.

Putting the Research to Use

It is important for inservice teacher educators to help interested classroom art teachers of artistically talented students become leaders who are empowered to make changes in their communities and in larger educational contexts. Teachers need to discover their own voices, develop senses of agency, take initiatives in response to challenges, and determine how and what they will teach in their classrooms. This study suggests a number of strategies, practiced in the Artistically Talented Program at Indiana University, that have proven successful for developing leadership skills for teachers of students with high ability in the visual arts. Once a group of teachers become leaders in their local schools, through collaboration and networking, they then can become mentors to other teachers and help build a community of teachers who in turn can effect changes in programming for artistically talented students at all levels.

THE ARTISTICALLY TALENTED PROGRAM

From 1990 to 1994, Gilbert Clark and I coordinated an Artistically Talented Program (ATP) at Indiana University (IU) supported through a contract with the Indiana Department of Education's Gifted and Talented Program. All teachers attending ATP were certified art teachers, accepted into the program on a competitive basis and required to be teaching in, or about to start, a program for talented visual arts students in their schools. They received scholarship support for room and board, tuition, supplies, and book expenses, as well as a stipend for purchasing art resources. Each summer the ATP teachers met for 2½ weeks; classes were offered in the mornings and afternoons. Approximately half the participants were returning and the other half were new participants. Although these art teachers took ATP courses at IU during the summer, they also had responsibilities to the program throughout the following school year. They were required to write and implement differentiated curricula designed for their local school settings, to keep a journal about their experiences teaching this curricula, to publish their curricula in a monograph disseminated throughout the state, to write short articles for an art education or gifted and talented magazine or journal about teaching their curricula, and to produce and present reports about their work at state gifted and talented conferences that focused on the visual arts. There was an emphasis on teachers choosing and developing themes for their curricula and then joining with three or four other ATP teachers to form cooperative teams for generating ideas and making presentations based on congruent interests (Thurber & Zimmerman, 1996). Every year, alumni from previous years met voluntarily to share ideas and to continue their previous networking and collaboration efforts.

METHODOLOGY

Two research studies were conducted with emphasis on the process and results of educating motivated teachers to become empowered and take leadership roles. One study involved focus groups of 1994 ATP participants; the other was a survey sent to all teachers who participated in ATP from 1991 to 1995.

Subjects

All 18 art teachers who attended the 1994 ATP met in three focus groups during the summer session to discuss issues relevant to the program. Information from their application forms indicated that prior to attending ATP, eight had taken courses or participated in workshops about artistically talented students; five had held leadership positions at local or state levels; three had received grants, scholarships, or other external funding; one had published an article in an art education magazine; and two had been named Teacher of the Year in their local schools. These visual art teachers were chosen on a competitive basis, and it was evident that they were interested in taking leadership roles in programs related to educating artistically talented students.

Eleven taught at the elementary level, two at the middle school level, and five at the high school level. Seven taught in urban areas (over 500,000 population), three in suburban schools (50,000 to 500,000 population), and eight in small towns (under 50,000 population). They had taught an average of 12 years, with a range between 2 and 23 years. There were 17 women and 1 man in the program: 16 were white and 2 were African American. Seven were returnees from the previous summer. The 1994 ATP teachers, like groups who preceded them, represented a wide range of ages, experiences, teaching situations, grade levels, and cultural, ethnic, and racial backgrounds. Their commonalities were that they were women art teachers (except one man) who would be teaching at least one class of artistically talented students in the fall of 1994. For 2 ½ weeks, these teachers lived on the same floor of a campus dormitory, took classes in the mornings and afternoons, participated in evening and weekend group activities, and ate three meals a day together in the dorm. Gilbert Clark and I, as directors of the program, taught the two ATP classes. We ate two meals a day with the teachers and attended almost all their extracurricular activities.

In 1995, we surveyed all 54 past participants of ATP, including the 18 who participated in the 1994 focus groups, to determine, whether over a five year period, they were able to become empowered and to maintain leadership positions in their schools and communities. Forty-six (90%) of the 54 participants responded; three surveys were returned due to lack of current addresses. Of the 46 teachers who returned surveys, 43 were women and 3 were men, 41 were white and 2 were African American, 22 were elementary art teachers, 18 were secondary art teachers, 3 were some combination of K-12 art teachers, and 1 taught at the college level. Four were not presently art teachers, but were teaching in other capacities. Seven taught in urban schools, 13 in suburban schools, and 26 in small rural schools.

Data Collection

All 18 teachers in the 1994 group participated in three focus groups; two consisted of new attendees and one of returnees. When members of these three groups were interviewed by the two directors, they were asked questions about their expectations for the program, their interactions with others in the program, whether and how ATP changed their approach to teaching, and their future plans when they returned to their local communities. Each focus group interview took place in a campus lounge, lasted for about two hours, and was recorded and transcribed. The survey form sent to all ATP alumni consisted of 11 questions that focused on their leadership roles, funding applied for or received, role changes in their schools, opportunities for artistically talented students they had created, published writings, initiatives in organizing art classes for high ability art students, their present positions, and effects of attending ATR.

Content analysis was used to categorize and analyze the transcriptions of the 1994 focus group discussions and the results of the survey administered in 1995 (see Gordon, 1978; Holsti, 1969; Mostyn, 1985). Because the questions asked in the focus groups were open-ended and not everyone responded, numbers reported do not necessarily reflect the point of view of every participant.

ATP PROGRAM OBJECTIVES

The ATP was designed specifically to educate inservice teachers about artistically talented students. The emphasis was on developing an understanding of problems, issues, and research related to identification, teaching methods and strategies, program policies, program evaluation, and educational resources designed for students who are gifted and talented in the visual arts. Participants were encouraged to reflect on their attitudes and values concerning the education of artistically talented students, and to formulate personal positions about programs for these students. Instruction also focused on helping the participants become aware of, and critically evaluate, curriculum resources and materials related to educating artistically talented students. In addition, ATP participants were encouraged, when they returned to their local schools, to observe, interact, present challenging themes and problems, and evaluate their high ability art students and help them develop to their full potential.

Other program objectives included assisting teachers to: (1) be challenged to think broadly, question their assumptions, and examine their own teaching strategies and interactions with their students; (2) introduce intellectually challenging and deliberately controversial content to their students; (3) develop their own agendas to determine what they needed to teach in their own local contexts; (4) become a community of teachers and inspire one another to become leaders in dissemination of ideas and practices for teaching artistically talented students; (5) form cooperative teams in which they explored thematic units based on their own interests and backgrounds; (6) be flexible and have broad ideas about what they would teach, but at the same time be willing to adjust or change topics and pace as their students required; and (7) assume leadership roles, write grants, exhibit their students' works, present their projects publicly at professional conferences, and publish about their experiences with these projects in educational magazines and in a monograph to be disseminated throughout the state.

STRATEGIES FOR INSTRUCTING ATP TEACHERS

The ATP classes focused on building a network of Indiana teachers who would not only be influencing their own talented art students, but also would be developing curricula and assessment to be shared with other teachers and students in their school corporations, at the state level, and in some cases nationally (Thurber & Zimmerman, 1996). Current course content, readings and materials relevant to understanding this content were high priorities. Emphasis was placed on researching topics of interest and using traditional means as well as new technologies to access materials.

There was a conscious attempt by the directors to create a family-like atmosphere by eating two meals a day with the teachers in the dorm where conversations ranged from problems and issues discussed in our classes to personal concerns and accomplishments. A substantial amount of time was spent in the evenings and on weekends participating in social and professional activities.

The teachers chose and developed their own themes and approaches to creating curricula for artistically talented students and then formed cooperative teams of three or four other teachers based on the similarities of their ideas. Titles of some of the thematic units developed through the program included: Boxes: Private and Public Spaces; Symbols in the Sand; The Human Figure as An Expressive, Symbolic Form; Art From the Earth; Ritual: From Prehistoric to Present Times; The Power of the Artist; Questions About Public Art; Birds in Flight; Metamorphosis of a Portrait; Folktales to Hear and See.

These teams continued to meet throughout the next academic year and some continued meeting three to four years after their formal ATP involvement ended. During the planning phase of creating thematic curricula, the teachers had access to an extensive art education library and were able to purchase resources and materials, with support from their scholarships. They also presented results of teaching these curricula to local, state, and national audiences. One ATP participant wrote after the class concluded: "We were able to build confidence in the ATP group so that we could go out and present our ideas and share them with our community and other teachers in the state." Yearly ATP alumni meetings take place, coordinated by the directors and past ATP participants, where new ideas are shared and successes celebrated.

FOCUS GROUPS

Questions asked of the teachers in the focus groups consisted of inquiries such as: (1) What were your expectations for ATP before you attended the program this summer? (2) What benefits, if any, did you receive from the course content, teaching strategies, resources, and field trips? (3) How did the living and dining arrangements, group activities, and studying with other teachers affect your participation in ATP? (4) How has participating in ATP changed your approach to teaching art to high ability students? (5) What are your future plans in respect to program activities for your artistically talented students? (6) What leadership roles in the area of education for your gifted and talented art students do you think you might assume during the coming academic year? Following are topics that emerged from content analysis of the focus group interviews. Example quotations from the 18 ATP teachers illustrate concepts that emerged from the data.

Knowledge of Subject Matter and Pedagogy

Ten of the teachers mentioned the great amount of information covered and the focus on methods that were current, timely, practical, and directly related to actual art classroom situations. What they learned in ATP connected directly with these teachers' own experiences and what they referred to as "real life situations." One teacher noted: "In ATP we didn't just develop theories, we had hands-on experiences that helped the theories make sense." Another observed: "People can hand you as many theories as they want, but if you do not know what is behind the theories, you are not going to understand what is happening."

Every teacher commented that the wide range of resources to which they had been introduced made them aware of many materials related to their curricular themes. Learning to use computerized data bases was a new skill for many and they felt that such knowledge would definitely be useful in the future. They expressed appreciation for the "package of goodies," instructional resources that the teachers were given based on their own choices. One teacher summarized many of the observations others made about the resources: "The resources are very valuable . . . enabling us to learn about resources we'd never have time to review, see, or buy on our own."

ATP teachers were committed to keeping current about professional practice. Twelve of the 18 teachers reported acquiring in-depth information about their subject matter, appreciated the materials they were given to read and discuss in classes, welcomed the ever-changing class contexts in respect to ways in which they were learning, and found the class content "thought provoking, and challenging." One teacher said: "This is a rigorous course of study . . . the research and conflicting ideas provided me with a knowledge base from which to proceed."

Problem solving, thinking sequentially, and developing thematic art units were mentioned by five of the teachers as valuable contributions to their professional development. One participant stated: "I learned how to take a big idea, break it down into parts, evaluate, rearrange, and eliminate parts to make something better . . . Now I am aware of curriculum balance . . . find a theme, create a sequence, make it meaningful, and include a relevant train of events." Developing an interdisciplinary approach, based on research and focused on effectively integrating art with other subjects, was viewed by 12 of the teachers as a positive aspect of the ATP.

All seven returning teachers reported that other teachers and their school administrators were supportive of their newly designed programs. Principals were especially impressed by their curriculum planning and the resources prepared by those who had made conference presentations the previous academic year. One returning teacher said: "It was great being accepted to speak . . . for a change somebody would be paying attention to me. I will not be seen only as someone in the corner making valentines."

Most teachers (16) reported that they gained knowledge and understanding of students with high ability and interest in the visual arts. They found out how to "watch for giftedness" and how to help artistically talented students "further their education through differentiated curriculum."

Self-Esteem

Participants had a number of expectations and preconceived notions about attending the program. Half had previous experiences with staff development courses; they expected to attend lectures and return to their dorm rooms to read. This was the first graduate course for one quarter of the teachers who, based on their undergraduate experiences, had reservations about returning to school and taking graduate level courses. Thirteen reported their expectations had been "exceeded by leaps and bounds." They indicated they learned a lot about identifying artistically talented students and accommodating their classroom needs. They also indicated that they learned a lot about themselves and the other teachers in the program.

Half the teachers reported feelings such as experiencing "tremendous surges of energy" and "excitement about returning to school and making changes."

Ten of the returning teachers reported that the excitement and energy they experienced in the program continued throughout the school year. One teacher explained that her students asked to stay after school to work on their art projects. "This even went on Friday after school when the students usually can't wait to go home . . . the whole school got involved in my program."

Four of the 11 new ATP teachers felt that they were not performing at the same level as others and lacked the growing confidence and self-esteem expressed by their classmates. One, a teacher from an inner city, confessed: "When you are teaching in an inner-city school your vocabulary starts to get diffused down into monosyllables and you feel as if you are very average and have to work really hard to keep up with everyone in the [ATP] program." When returning ATP teachers presented the curricula they taught the previous academic year, four of the new participants felt intimidated and overwhelmed by the materials and information being presented. One moment they felt empowered and anxious to make changes and at the next moment they felt frustrated and lacked confidence. One confided: "I felt like I was an inch tall . . . Part of ATP is so overwhelming, you just want to get up and leave." At the conclusion of the ATP three of these four teachers reported that they felt more comfortable and gained "an in-depth understanding of myself and what I teach." One was still concerned whether she would be able to do all that was expected of her.

Collaboration

Elements of "human connection" were viewed as salient to success of the program. All teachers mentioned that the most valuable and rewarding aspects of ATP were the family-like environment, emphasis on caring and networking, and sharing of information among the participants. Of the seven teachers from rural areas, six mentioned that they generally felt isolated and found that being with a community of teachers provided a support network lacking in their local school districts. Most of the elementary level art specialist teachers, who were the only art teachers in their schools, reported they enjoyed being with others with similar interests and abilities. One participant likened the nurturing she was receiving at ATP to good parenting: "This is the kind of learning done at home at the dinner table having conversation. That is where you get your values and intuitive learning . . . this is the ideal learning situation." Another expressed her concern that the idea of care is not always evident in educational endeavors: "The caring unit has been destroyed in society and we are reestablishing it here. Then we can take it back to our classrooms. The students need it and crave it."

Communal living in the dorm produced excitement about being art educators, feelings of camaraderie, and interactions in terms of emotional and intellectual support. One participant explained: "The best thing was the ability to talk to other people and live with them . . . to see each other with our hair messed and toothpaste coming out of our mouths . . . you have to become more intimate." Another added: "Our conversations would begin as soon as we were conscious in the morning, go through breakfast, and continue until we went to bed at night." Networking and sharing ideas was a new and energizing experience for the 11 teachers who previously had not participated in this type of intense interaction. One participant pondered: "People in the business world network professionally . . . why don't teachers do that? . . . we all want to improve ourselves, our students, and our school systems."

Empowerment and Leadership

All returning teachers described how they shared their experiences with peers, administrators, and communities when they taught the previous year. Seven noted that they were the first teachers from their rural schools to speak at a state or national conference and the acclamation and visibility they received for their art programs was invaluable. Most mentioned displaying their students' art works at places outside their local communities. All returning teachers described leadership roles they had taken at local and state levels. A typical example of a teacher's reactions to taking a new leadership role follows: "I was asked to be on the state education commission for arts grants . . . I wouldn't have agreed to serve if I hadn't gone to ATP and felt confident in saying what I thought was important."

Building bridges between school art programs and local communities was another theme that emerged from focus groups' responses. Educating students, parents, and school administrators about art was a new concern for eight teachers. One observation was that: "Once parents and administrators are made part of the art program by involving them and informing them of happenings in the art class, wonderful things can happen."

Self-reflection, empowerment, personal growth, and emerging leadership roles were themes repeated and elaborated upon by the teachers. Reflection was mentioned in terms of problem solving, new ways of approaching curriculum construction, past teaching practices, and innovative ways of delivering material to their students. Fourteen of the teachers expressed feeling a sense of empowerment and confidence they thought would lead to making changes in their programs for artistically talented students. One teacher explained the breadth of her empowerment: "I now feel I can go out and present ideas as yearly themes that focus on my needs and those of my students and share them with our community and other teachers in the state." A returning teacher explained how her feelings of empowerment affected her teaching when she returned to school: "I walked into my class of talented art students feeling empowerment . . . I was in charge. I had a plan and it was going to be executed . . . the principal cooperated and the teachers started noticing. The kids started responding. Art was no longer on the back burner. It was noticed."

One returning teacher used a metaphor of combat to express her positive reactions to attending ATP the previous summer: "When you teach you get dents in your armor and you get defensive . . . You come here with others in your field. You polish your armor and hammer out all the dents so that you can go back and teach." Four of the seven returning teachers recognized that, during their first summer, they had been mentored by the previous years' attendees. They, in turn, helped new 1994 participants get acclimated to the program, served as resource persons, and answered questions based on their previous summer's experiences. One returning teacher observed: "I look at the diverse group this year and the variety of their backgrounds and I see everyone moving from a naive to sophisticated state to some degree, although the nature of the states are (sic) different."

Things That Need to Be Changed

Not every aspect of the ATP was positive. Teachers, especially art teachers, are not used to sitting and listening to verbal explanations about subject matter and participating in pedagogical discussions about teaching. Their relationship to their students often is in a studio-like environment where they move around and critique art works. It is rare that they have time to do demonstrations and even rarer that they conduct looking and talking about art lessons. About one quarter of the participants found it difficult to sit in class for three hours in the morning and three more in the afternoon. Many wanted more time to use resources, and most importantly, more time to reflect about what they had learned. University level instructors often forget that classroom teachers are not used to the environment found in many higher education institutions. Adult students should be allowed sufficient time to use resources and reflect upon what they are learning. One expressed her needs this way: "We have all these things spinning around in our heads. I wish we had more time to think about all the things we learned because it is hard to go home to a normal life after this intense experience.

SURVEY RESULTS

In response to the first of 11 questions on the survey about *what leadership positions they had been offered or held since they had attended ATP*, 36 of the 46 alumni who responded had held numerous leadership positions at school, community, higher education, state, and national levels. At the school level, 16 chaired, directed, or coordinated various visual arts activities including a school musical; an outdoor environmental laboratory; and curriculum, gifted and talented, assessment, business, teachers' contract, and computer committees. At the community level, four were members of community arts councils and district-wide art identification and curriculum committees, eight belonged to broad-based planning committees; three headed school corporation-museum advisory committees, two served on the board of regional art alliances, one was a member of a textbook adoption committee; one directed a student art gallery and another a school corporation art show.

At the higher education level, one served as an evaluator for a federal grant, another directed a summer art program, two taught college classes in elementary art methods, and two were invited university speakers. At the state and national levels, they served in 13 different leadership positions on the board of the Art Education Association of Indiana (AEAI) that ranged from three conference coordinators to three presidents; four served as members of the Indiana Art Standards Committee; four were members of the state gifted and talented cadre; one was on the board of a state arts organization; two were on the boards of national art competitions.

In question 2 on the survey, 37 teachers responded about *scholarships, fellowships, grants, or other funding they applied for and/or received after attending ATP.* Three applied for, but did not receive funding from different agencies. At the school level, other teachers received six internal funding stipends, two grants for revising art curricula, three summer grants for teaching art classes, one Schools 2000 grant, and three PTO mini-grants. Eleven wrote, and nine received, mini-grants from their school corporations, three received grants from community organizations to create murals, and others received grants to have students study local architecture or create a permanent large-scale sculpture. At the state level, ATP participants received 30 gifted and talented mini-grants, 2 technology grants, 3 Very Special Arts grants and 4 arts and/or teacher foundation grants, and 3 participated in an international exchange program. At the national level, ATP teachers received four study scholarships (Council for Basic Education, Chicago Arts Institute, Frank Lloyd Wright Foundation, and Wal-Mart) and a Getty Center for Education in the Arts doctoral research fellowship.

Thirty-two teachers responded to question 3 about *role changes they experienced in their schools or districts since they attended ATP.* They described being recognized as resource persons for conducting workshops and doing private consultancies, taking leadership roles as department chairpersons and chairing local educational committees, serving as a school grants coordinator, changing their positions in their schools and districts, becoming a college professor, and establishing artistically talented programs in their schools. Four mentioned new levels of administrative support for their art programs. One wrote: "I am no longer an institutionalized baby sitter."

Thirty-five responded to question 4 about *classes, programs, or other opportunities for artistically talented students they created, taught, administered, or coordinated after attending ATP.* Thirty reported creating artistically talented classes during school time, two reported class taught by local artists during the school day, two established independent study art classes, seven started after-school or Saturday art programs for high ability art students, one taught early morning art enrichment classes, five incorporated differentiated curricula into regular art classes, and eight initiated summer art classes. Other opportunities included two teachers who created national art honor societies, three who arranged field trips, five whose students created art works for their local communities, and thirteen whose students exhibit annually in community and university art centers.

Twenty responded to question 5 about *authoring or publishing articles, reports, or other writings in local or other newspapers, magazines, journals, district publications, or other sources.* Seventeen wrote articles published in local newspapers or newsletters, and eight reported coverage in local newspapers in articles written by others. Articles by nine appeared in national educational magazines and journals. One wrote a master's practicum and another a doctoral dissertation based on concepts and ideas learned at ATP.

In question 6, forty-three reported *initiatives they have taken since attending ATP in originating, revising, or adapting differentiated curricula and/or learning activities to accommodate to the needs of high ability visual arts students.* Fifteen wrote and implemented individualized thematic units of instruction; three provided more options within units of instruction; seven individualized their units of instruction for all students even though they did not have special artistically talented classes; four initiated visiting artists and guest speakers programs; five introduced computer art programs and five initiated interdisciplinary art programs. Other initiatives included five teachers establishing artistically talented programs; four initiating independent study programs for high school students identified as artistically talented, one establishing an international baccalaureate program, and four participating in portfolio assessment programs. In addition, four established after school programs, one established a children's art gallery, and another had art materials added to the academically gifted and talented students' resource room in her school.

All respondents answered question 7 on the survey that addressed *personal effects on teacher attitudes, involvement, student relations, professional career, personal relationships, career aspirations, etc. as a result of attending the ATP and interacting with other ATP participants.* The most frequent response, mentioned by 21 participants, was networking with other teachers that continues to the present. Eleven teachers wrote that ideas and concepts discussed and practiced at ATP changed the way they construct their curricula; the same number responded that ATP changed the way they teach and view teaching. Nine noted that they gained greater self-confidence than they had before attending ATP. Six individuals responded that they publicize their art programs at school, community, and state levels, focus their energies in a more positive direction than before, and are now convinced of the need for a discipline-based art education approach to teaching. Other responses reflected ways in which they had become involved in local and statewide leadership, including attending and presenting at professional meetings; developing positive relationships between teachers, administrators, and arts professionals at their schools; and being looked to in their school district for new ideas in gifted and talented education. Six respondents credit going on to receive advanced degrees as directly influenced by attending ATP. As one person stated, "I have to do things, not just complain, and I have become more professionally involved."

Question 8 on the survey, that asked *since attending ATP, what effects, rewards, and accomplishments of their students they could report,* was responded to by 44 teachers. Eighteen mentioned art exhibits at the school, community, or state levels, and 16 wrote that their students won more art competitions (e.g. Symphony in Color, poster contests, and National Scholastic Awards) than before they attended ATP. Twelve responses referred to the fact that their students now are willing to take risks and are accomplishing and learning more than in the past and that they are aware of and appreciate the art found in their local communities. Six of their students were reported to have won scholarships and four had examples of their artwork published in local newspapers. Five individual responses cited increased enrollment in their art departments, going on field trips to museums and galleries for the first time, and establishing mentoring programs for their students with local artists.

Survey question 9 addressed *how attending IU ATP contributed to their work and accomplishments described in question eight*. There were 44 responses. The most frequent, reported by 13 respondents, was support, networking, information, and guidance that was offered by other teachers. A dozen responses were found in each of the following categories: ATP provided knowledge and support that enabled them to pursue meaningful theory and practice; as a result of attending ATP, their art curricula now is more comprehensive, sequential, and thematic; and they gained personal confidence, courage, and self-esteem that enabled them to do what they needed and wanted to do. Seven responses indicated that participation made them enthusiastic about teaching; they now apply what they learned at ATP to teaching artistically talented students, and they use the knowledge they learned in ATP to get funds and publicity for their programs. Other responses that four or more people addressed were: learning how to use discipline-based art education methods, including authentic assessments, in their art programs; exploring a variety of resources, meeting their students' needs more effectively, being more professional, setting goals, and following through and gaining their colleagues' respect; and sharing, growing, and risk taking that they continue to the present. Ten cited the support offered by the instructors as role models that continues to be important in their everyday activities in their art classrooms.

Question 10 concerned *what position they held when they first entered ATP, what position they now hold, and what initiatives they were working on at the time of the survey*. All 46 respondents answered the three parts of this question. Twenty-six wrote they originally were elementary art teachers, five were gifted and talented coordinators, seven were middle school art teachers, eight were high school art teachers, two were middle school art department chairpersons, three were high school art department chairpersons, and three were instructors of college art methods classes. Others were a computer teacher at the elementary level, a K-12 art teacher, a high school drama coach, and an art teacher in a school for the deaf.[1]

Thirty-six hold the same positions as when they entered the ATP program. Four were in the same school districts but changed the grade levels and/or schools in which they were teaching. Seven held new positions as a regular K-6 art teacher, a district gifted and talented coordinator, a high school art teacher in another school corporation, a department chair in a private high school, a school corporation resource teacher, a head of a school multiculture program, and a university art educator (see note 1).

In response to gifted and talented initiatives in which they presently were involved, 3 reported they had no gifted and talented art programs in their schools, 3 others wrote they were not involved in new initiatives, and 24 described a bevy of programs they were initiating for artistically talented students as well as other students in their schools.[2] Other initiatives included responses from 25 teachers who indicated they were involved in early morning, after-school, Saturday Art, pull-out, and independent study programs, as well as art clubs during the school day and summer art programs. Fourteen were differentiating their art curricula, 10 were working with community members to create art projects for their schools and their local communities, and 5 were educating and collaborating with others in their schools in special programs for artistically talented students.[3]

In the last question, teachers were asked *whether there were additional initiatives, accomplishments, or role-changes they wished to report or any additional comments they wanted to make*. Thirty-nine responded to this question citing their own accomplishments, including one teacher who was nominated three times by her students to be included in *Who's Who Among America's Teachers*. Another was named AEAI Secondary Art Teacher of the Year, a third was named by her school corporation as art teacher of the year, and a fourth was recognized as one of the most influential teachers in her school by vote of ten top academic students. Three were named Inland-Steel-Ryerson Foundation Teachers of the Year, and three have received Lilly Foundation Teacher Creativity Fellowships.

Three expressed frustration at not being able to initiate artistically talented programs in their schools because of lack of administrative support. This was not the case with most, however, who responded that the support they were receiving from their administrators was positive. One wrote, "The administration and staff have commented on my students' achievements in art with great enthusiasm and respect." Another wrote that "We are now going on tours, holding community art exhibits, and I am dialoging (sic) with my students in new ways."

Teachers of Talented Art Students in Leadership Roles

Instruction in ATP focused on content, teaching strategies, and future empowerment for inservice art teachers who had interest and motivation to become leaders in the area of educating artistically talented students. A framework emerged, however, from generalizations based on content analysis of the data from the focus groups and from the survey results that also may have applicability to other inservice education programs for teachers of talented art students. It appears that knowledge of subject matter content and pedagogy, building self-esteem, and allowing choices may lead teachers of artistically talented students, who have a desire to take leadership roles, to collaborate with others and eventually become empowered to make changes in their private and professional lives. These changes eventually result in communities of caring teachers who are able to assume new leadership roles in their schools, communities, and state organizations. In comparing ATP to successful teacher inservice programs studied by Maeroff (1988), the program had many characteristics he described. Such programs produced teachers who were engaged in studying the content and teaching of their subject matter and who bonded and continued relationships with other participants after the summer program ended. A community of teachers, as advocated by Lieberman and McLaughlin (1992) and Darling-Hammond (1993), was established among the participants. Many ATP alumni are what Sprague (1992) described as "activists" in local and state communities for artistically talented students and are regarded as valuable professionals no longer sitting in a corner cutting out valentines.

Based on the focus group interviews and survey responses, it appears that most objectives set by the program were met by an overwhelming majority of the participants. Most ATP participants were women and this experience, as they reported, aided most of them to find their own voices, to speak loudly and be heard. Many held leadership positions at local and state levels, received numerous scholarships, awards, and grants, created new programs for their artistically talented students, published articles, reports, or other writings about artistically talented students, adapted curricula based on the needs of these students, and reported other personal and professional accomplishments.

ATP alumni had positive effects on art programs for talented students in their local communities, as well as facilitating building communities of teachers across the state, the impact of which was felt by students, colleagues, parents, administrators, and local community members. The majority of these art teachers gained knowledge about art content and teaching artistically talented students, achieved feelings of self-esteem, collaborated with others, and became caring and empowered leaders who made positive changes in their classrooms, communities, school corporations, at the state level and beyond.

NOTES

1. Some held more than one of these positions.

2. These included XL Art, Enrichment Triad, School Art Gallery, Apprentice Guild, High Achievers, Visual and Performing Arts Program, G/T Visionaries, Art Benefactors' Club, Artists in Residence, Project ARTS, Extended Learning, Portfolio Prep Class, and Honors Club.

3. Some were involved in more than one initiative.

REFERENCES

Darling-Hammond, L. D. (1993). Reframing the school reform agenda: Developing capacity for school transformation. *Phi Delta Kappan, 74*, 753–761.

Galbraith, L. (Ed.). (1995). *Preservice art education issues and practice.* Reston, VA: National Art Education Association.

Gordon, W. I. (1978). *Communication: Personal and public.* New York: Alfred.

Holsti, O. R. (1969). *Content analysis for the social sciences and humanities.* Reading, MA: Addison.

Lieberman, A., & McLaughlin, M. W. (1992). Networks for educational change: Powerful and problematical. *Phi Delta Kappan, 73*, 673–677.

Maeroff, G. I. (1988). A blueprint for empowering teachers. *Phi Delta Kappan, 69*, 473–477.

Mostyn, B. (1985). The content analysis of qualitative research data: A dynamic approach. In M. Brenner, J. Brown, & D. Canter (Eds.), *The research interview: Uses and approaches* (pp. 115–145). London: Academic Press.

Sprague, J. (1992). Critical perspectives on teacher empowerment. *Communication Education, 41*, 181–200.

Thurber, F., & Zimmerman, E. (1996). Empower not in power: Gender and leadership issues in art education. In G. Collins & R. Sandell (Eds.), *Gender issues in art education* (pp. 114–153). Reston, VA: National Art Education Association.

Zimmerman, E. (1994). Current research and practice about preservice visual arts specialist teacher education. *Studies in Art Education, 35*, 79–89.

Zimmerman, E. (in press). Whence come we? What are we? Whither go we? Demographic analysis of art teacher preparation programs in the United States. In M. Day (Ed.), *Profiles for art teacher preparation.* Reston, VA: National Art Education Association.

Index

Note: References to tables or figures are indicated by *italic type* and the addition of *"t"* or *"f"* respectively.

CORWIN PRESS

The Corwin Press logo—a raven striding across an open book—represents the union of courage and learning. Corwin Press is committed to improving education for all learners by publishing books and other professional development resources for those serving the field of K–12 education. By providing practical, hands-on materials, Corwin Press continues to carry out the promise of its motto: **"Helping Educators Do Their Work Better."**